Library and Archives Canada Cataloguing in Publication

Gibson, Shane, 1975-
Closing bigger : the field guide to closing bigger business deals / Shane Gibson with Trevor Greene.

ISBN 0-9738174-0-2

1. Selling. I. Greene, Trevor II. Title.

HF5438.25.G545 2005 658.85 C2005-902809-2

This book is dedicated to our children

Kristian Gibson

And

Grace Greene

TABLE OF CONTENTS

"Shane Gibson, ably aided by Trevor Greene, has made a rare contribution to the body of sales wisdom: a book that leads you on a cellular level through the process of surmounting lofty financial peaks, yet a book that reads as gently as a stroll in the park. If you are willing to work hard enough to be your own miracle, Closing Bigger will illuminate the path for you."

Jay Conrad Levinson
The father of guerrilla marketing
Author, Guerrilla Marketing series of books
Over 14 million sold; now in 41 languages
www.gmarketing.com
www.guerrillamarketingassociation.com

"There has been much written about selling, negotiating and closing deals and I think I've read them all. Closing Bigger gives you the process that can take you from small time to the big league. If you are seriously committed to closing big deals, then this book is a MUST READ!"

Dr. Denis L. Cauvier
Best selling author,
The ABC's of Making Money
www.abcsofmakingmoney.com

"Thanks Shane…I closed over $700,000 worth of business within 45 days after reading your book, this would have normally taken me 6 months to pull off"!

Chad Rissanen
www.jettmarketing.com

Acknowledgements

There are many people who were invaluable in helping us write this book. We would like to name a few of them here, especially Bill Gibson, mentor and father, whose methodologies and vast experience formed the foundation for the principles in this book.

We also thank our mentors from all walks of life and experience:

- Dr. Denis Cauvier, who pushed us to take this book to market and shared his wealth of knowledge and experience in the publishing arena.

- Robert Palkowski, lawyer, father figure and street fighter who has always been in our corner.

- Nigel Horsley, the consummate PR practitioner who told us to go big or go home.

- Peter Thomas and Jay Levinson, for their leap of faith in putting their names and personal brands behind this book.

- Our local business community, particularly the entire team at the Vancouver Board of Trade, for your belief, support and positive buzz about Closing Bigger.

- Jonathan Lam, our very own e-genius.

- Craig Young for his deft design and layout creativity.

- Our big deal closers: Lisa Howell, Dak Molnar, Willi Schmidt and Carey Healey, and our subject matter experts: Nick Usborne, Jim Janz and Michael Barker-Fyfe.

- And finally, to everyone in our Closing Bigger community, going for the brass ring and daring to dream big.

Foreword

by Peter H. Thomas

In my early years of selling I could definitely have used this book. I have always argued that selling is not an art but a science. There is no doubt in my mind that anyone utilizing the systems explained in this book on the science of closing sales will earn substantially higher income much more quickly than without the book.

It is said that nothing happens until someone sells something to somebody. Shane tells you how to close those sales. This book cuts away all the myths and gets right down to the basics. In a very easy and understandable format, he tells you how to be successful in closing sales. It is a step by step system that will work.

Peter H. Thomas
Founder, Century 21 Real Estate Canada
Chairman, Board of Advisors, Young Entrepreneurs Organization
Director, World Presidents' Organization

Preface

The idea to write a book on closing bigger business deals didn't come about from a brainstorming session, or an impulse to put a new spin on an old topic in order to sell a lot of books. There are a lot of exceptional books out there on selling but Trevor and I found that few directly addressed closing big deals. We decided to answer a question voiced by many of our clients: how do I become a big deal closer?

First we had to figure out what exactly constitutes a big deal. For a small-business person, a big deal may be a $10,000 sale, when their average sale is $1,000. For real estate giant Colliers International, a big deal is closed when one of their commercial realtors sells a city block for $100 million. We have decided to draw the line at $1 million. From talking to both buyers and sellers, there seems to be a psychological shift attached to the $1 million-plus level. Plus, you rarely hear people referring to the $900,000-aire next door. In business, social and tax circles, millionaires and million-dollar deals are recognized as icons. Many of the big-deal closers we spoke to like to say that their first million dollars were the hardest to make.

It is an honor to have Peter H. Thomas write the foreword for the book. Many years ago when I began my career in selling I spent an entire week poring over Peter's books and tapes on selling, and what I heard still influences the way I sell and relate to business people today. Just to clarify, throughout the book, the pronoun "I" refers to Shane Gibson. "We" refers to the entire team at Knowledge Brokers International.

In writing the book, Trevor and I interviewed many dealmakers both informally and formally. We couldn't put all of the interviews in the book so we chose four distinct conversations.

These interviews in their entirety can be found in the chapter titled "The Closers." Despite their different backgrounds and industries, each of these four big deal closers embodied the strategies that we talk about in the book. These interviews confirmed for us that our process for closing big deals is being used right now, everywhere.

While we were working on Closing Bigger, we shared our vision and progress with pretty much everyone with whom we came into contact. We found that nearly everyone had a big deal closer that we "just had to meet."

We weren't able to meet everyone that we should have, but all of the big deal closers that we did have the opportunity to talk to had their own unique story to tell about closing big deals. Most of them learned their trade through mentorship and osmosis, while some of them got to the summit painfully through trial and error. This book will hopefully be your short cut to big deal closer status. Lisa, Dak, Carey and Willi from "The Closers" chapter are your mentors. Hang on every word they say. It is our hope that the lessons and experiences they share, along with the blueprint for closing big deals laid out in this book, is your path to the peak of your industry.

Shane Gibson, with Trevor Greene

"Faith is taking the first step
even when you don't see
the whole staircase.

Martin Luther King, Jr."

Introduction

I delivered a seminar a few years ago to the Vancouver-based British Columbia Technology Industries Association on sales for non-salespeople. I asked this room of chief technology officers and tech-industry executives to define selling for me. After a while, one table came up with the following statement: "Sales is about being nice to someone you may not like, in an attempt to sell them something they probably don't need."

I considered that statement as I shared with them my preferred definition: selling is creating an environment where an act of faith can take place.

Faith is based on trust and trust is built on credibility.

This book is about improving the toolkit you need to close big deals, how to improve your prowess as a big deal maker and the process of closing on a big deal. That process is not about buying, it's about buy-IN. And buy-in is all about faith, trust and credibility.

For example, if you are buying a cellphone, you don't ask about how the chips inside the cellphone were made, or how the frequencies were selected based on extensive research you have done. No. You are assuming because of the faith you have in the individual and the company that all of these things have been taken care of. You have, essentially, bought on faith.

Closing big deals is like closing smaller deals, except there is more at stake. The risk affects not just the buyer and seller but also entire companies and possibly hundreds of employees. Imagine if you were buying 10,000 cell phones, how much more faith and credibility you would need from the vendor. What if a bad purchase made by you results in your boss firing you or hurting your ability to advance in the company? That is the level of faith we are talking about in big deals. You are putting the livelihood of your company in the hands of the vendor.

With all due regards to the British Columbia Technology Industries Association, they were actually instrumental in planting the seed for this book by requesting that I address the topic of closing big deals in the format of a keynote speech for their member base. They identified this as one of the common challenges that high tech, complex solution providers face across the globe.

The one thing you need to know about closing on big deals is...there is more than one thing you need to know.

Shane Gibson,
Vancouver, June 2005

"...often the only difference between us and the competitor is that we have a better relationship with the client."

- Shane Gibson

I.
The Three Levels of Sales

As the model below shows, there are three levels of sales. First is *transactional* or *order-taking,* usually based on small or commodity-based sales. The second level is relationship-based, where a level of rapport and trust needs to be built. On this level, often the only difference between us and the competitor is that we have a better relationship with the client. Most people sell using a combination of first and second level selling skills. This book is about helping you identify what it's going to take to move your selling to the third level.

The third level of selling encompasses partnership selling, consultative selling and needs analysis selling. Third level selling is where 98% of big deals are closed.

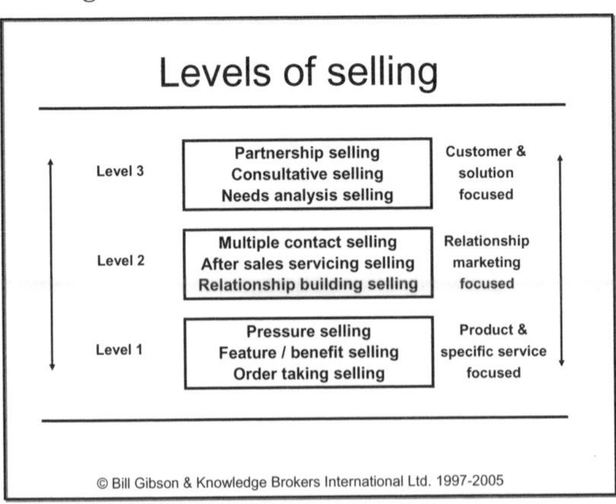

An Overview of Third-Level Selling Skills

Be a multiple relationship manager

In order to close and sustain big deals you need to be a multiple relationship manager. This is an individual who looks at all the people connected to the buyer on the client side as well as all the people on his/her team. A conductor of sorts, this manager plans and executes maneuvers, is a politician, a connector and translator all in tandem.

Be an information gatherer

As a big deal closer you also have to identify what the prospective buyer needs and wants. Keep an ear to the jungle telegraph that resonates in your market. It is there if you have ears to hear it, giving you the gossip, the new trends, the power plays and all the power shifts. This unofficial "street MBA" hotline will give you the informal knowledge you need to supplement the traditional channels of communication and strategic-account acquisition plans.

Be a master of follow-up and follow-through

As you can see from the statistics below, being a master of follow-up and follow-through is critical to gaining new clients, particularly when we are converting them from existing suppliers. The return is exponential once the fourth contact is made when contacting a competitor's clients.

Sales conversion ratio

(On calls made to 100 competitors' clients)

Your Calls	Converted	Percentage
1st	2 of 100	2%
2nd	3 of 98	3%
3rd	4 of 95	4%
4th	10 of 91	10%
5th and onward	81 of 81	81%

"It could take 50 calls to convert # 81"

An average salesperson will make two calls and then quit. This means they have about 3% of the potential business on their prospect list. If you want to hit a home run you need to be willing to push on and make those five to 12 contacts to convert the 81% of the potential business in the market.

It is not about just picking up the phone and asking the client if they are ready to buy yet. It is about adding value to a clients' day without harassing them with constant requests to buy. Mix your contact methods between e-mails, phone calls, personal faxes, drop-in visits, share industry-related how-to articles, tips and newsletters, invites for coffee, even have your CEO call the client. I have heard many times that on the third contact with someone, they trust you 70% more. So, if your whole team is in contact with them your whole company has the opportunity to develop that level of trust.

Know when to close

Another key factor to closing big deals is knowing when to close. There are both verbal and non-verbal buying signals, and they can come at any time. Some buying signals come when the client asks questions about what happens after the purchase or what kind of after-sales support they get. They may also be mentally in the process of buying, for instance by asking about terms of payment or training for their staff on your product. They may look back at a product, proposal or brochure several times, asking detailed but positive questions. At a non-verbal level, a receptive buyer can have a change in attitude and body language, like when they open up and start smiling, possibly spring for lunch or talk about referrals.

If you can't close the deal, at least close the next step

The key factor is to make arrangements to set up the next step or appointment. Book it right then and there. If you can't close the deal, make sure you have closed something before you leave. Book the next appointment; get a commitment on a next step that you know will keep the prospect hot and you top of mind.

II.

Eight Big Deal Breakers

Here is a set of guidelines that great salespeople follow to blow deals. As you read this section, you may become aware that you have probably committed one or more of these.

I call these guidelines and not rules because there are always exceptions. You may need to violate one of these guidelines to close a deal. Just be aware of the risk it represents.

Research: there's none or it's old

One way to break a deal is to assume that the prospect is just like everyone else in the industry, or that their business challenge and direction has stayed the same since you last visited them six months ago. The reality is, their reality has likely changed.

One buyer for a well-known outdoor-goods chain said he used to be amazed at how the sellers to whom he gave the magic 15 minutes of his time would squander the chance.

"I was the guy who was empowered to write the $2 million cheque. These people would sit in my office and I would be shaking my head on the inside because it was clear that they hadn't researched the ethics or founding principles of my company, or they had prepped a pitch that was years out of date," he said. "They literally hadn't taken the time and effort to re-research the pitch. They just dusted off the old one."

One of the ways we can ensure that we are not acting on old or bad research is to use a needs analysis approach to our prospects or existing clients if we are not 100% sure of our data and assumptions.

Needs analysis makes the salesperson listen to the client and opens the client to explore aspects they hadn't thought of before. Pertinent questions are addressed instead of being missed, and the client is led to think about solutions in way that enables the team to explore applications.

A needs analysis also serves as a record for future dealings with that client, and forms an information base for support staff. It puts the focus on the customer and elevates the salesperson to the level of a trusted advisor, versus that of a product or service peddler.

Conducting a needs analysis provides education about a real company in the real world. Do a needs analysis for 50 different companies in an industry and you will be an expert on that industry.

While your competitors are taking orders and viewing opportunities in the market through a filter of ignorance, you will be able to see the big picture, anticipate client needs and even provide leadership to your clients in your area of expertise. You may even get to know their industry and competitors better than they do.

Needs analysis forces the seller to listen to the client, makes the customer think and explore new options, ensures that pertinent questions aren't missed and that sales points are suggested and tied to the answer.

And, most vitally, it leads the client to think about all the applications of your offering to their business. It leads them to discover themselves that what you have on offer is viable – even critical – to their business. They widen their vision to see multiple solutions you can bring to their business. You can also uncover unmet needs they didn't know they had.

I did a needs analysis for leadership training at a large insurance company. But what came out was further contracts for key account sales training, communications training and call-centre training. Through this process, the client themselves came to the conclusion that they needed more. The proposal was a formality, nothing more than a confirmation of what they told me they needed. By the time the needs analysis was done, I had won the deal.

If we were to go back to that client today and ask if I had actually sold them anything, they would say no. They knew I hadn't sold them. We had simply uncovered their real needs and fulfilled them.

You may find that the needs analysis indicates that there is not a fit between your company and the prospective client. There, you have an excellent opportunity to build credibility by referring the client to a competitor. When you refer them to a better-suited vendor you build a high level of credibility and, in my experience, this creates the potential for a strong long-term relationship.

The needs analysis is built on a foundation of intelligent questions, which show competence and knowledge. They build trust and show concern. About 80% of your vital knowledge will come from 20% of the questions you ask.

These intelligent questions demonstrate that you are a professional; they show your competence, build trust and prove to the client that you are concerned about their needs.

During the needs analysis, it is important to never sell or pitch the client. Simply assess. If you try to sell during this phase, the client will see this as an underhanded tactic and you will lose credibility. Furthermore, if they feel sold to, they will stop sharing valuable info. In fact they may give you misinformation as a defense measure against your insincere tactics.

Using a needs analysis approach you really get to know the clients':

✓ Likes	✓ Fears
✓ Problems	✓ Dreams
✓ Objectives	✓ Goals
✓ Dislikes	✓ Beliefs
✓ Achievements	✓ Challenges
✓ Values	✓ Motivations

No fit = referral = credibility = referral

Starting with the wrong person

Deal with the true decision-maker. Don't start halfway up the company or at a middle manager. The crawl up the ladder is painful if you start too low. I don't want to give the impression that these people aren't important or valuable. The reality is, too many people in the middle ranks let on that they have more influence, "go" power and authority than they actually have.

Take the somewhat quirky analogy of the fire in the office building lobby. Someone on the ground floor calls the mid-level to say there is a fire raging. The mid level executives tell senior management that there are fire trucks downstairs, and the CEO hears that someone somewhere smells smoke.

Aim high for the core decision maker; it is worth it. Even if they refer you to a subordinate, make sure you ask permission of the decision maker to keep them in the communications loop. The reason is we constantly want to make sure that we are connected and communicating with the real power base. This will give a better posture with subordinates and ensure that the solution doesn't diverge from the core values of the leader.

If you get your message to the top ranks with power and impact, there will be no dilution along the way and no other agendas will have been added. Also, many middle managers are terrified to take the risk of endorsing you and your product to the brass, for fear of making a wrong call. Top execs are there to take risks and make decisions. They are the people with yes-power.

Even though top execs cut cheques and hold real power, there are still likely to be many people in the client organization who can affect the decision makers' opinions, and could even adversely affect how well your solution is implemented after the deal is closed.

Avoid the temptation to get too comfortable and rely solely on your relationship with the decision maker. The more complex the deal, the more people that have to get involved, and all have valuable perspectives and contributions to bring to your deal.

Bear in mind that your decision maker may get transferred or fired, and then you are left to deal with a whole corporate power structure that you have neglected.

A few years ago in South Africa, KBI Chairman Bill Gibson built a system for big deals involving long sales cycles, called the Managing Complex Business Relationships System. The system was used by major South African banks as well as by the energy and industry division of giant multinational Siemens. Bill put the program together with a specific focus on how to sell through the power network, or as you may know it, the corporate power structure. After evaluating this network, he found that there are six main power players in every corporate power network.

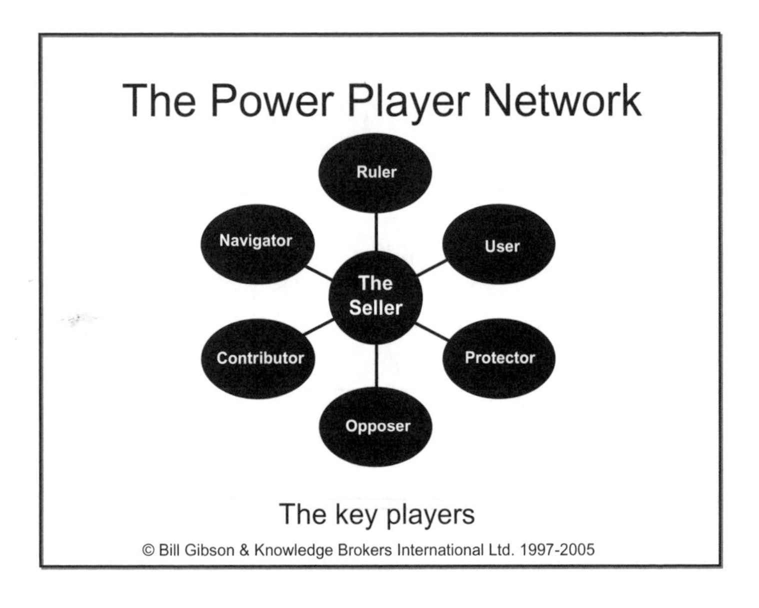

The Rulers. Bottom-line oriented and attuned to the benefits of the deal. You generally get one shot at these people. Some rulers tend to work by consensus, while others rule by command and control. Your mission is to figure out how the ruler rules, and either build a positive consensus among the ruler's team or get very proactive and draw them a map in a dynamic 30 seconds. The ruler can also be a small group that makes the final decision together.

The Navigators. Can discuss office politics and the key players and know who else is bidding on the contract. They could be senior salespeople from another division, for example. But the navigator won't sell on your behalf and certainly won't stick their neck out for you. They will be on your side if they feel that you are in the best interests of the company. They know information is power and are very well aware that they hold powerful information. They will talk to you and help you out because they feel that you have what the company wants. You can find and meet navigators in informal settings like golf games and association meetings. You engage them by appealing to their interests, values and maybe their ego.

The Users. The people actually using your product or service on a hands-on basis. They can sabotage the deal if they feel it is being crammed down their throats. They are looking at how the deal affects their job. Having users on your side can be a huge benefit. If there is a positive buzz throughout the office on all levels about your solution, it is very difficult for other power players to implement a competing agenda.

The Protectors. Usually found in departments like R&D, legal, accounting or HR. They are often jockeying to gain more buying power within the network. [The reason for this is they are often acting on behalf of another person or department – in other words, they are involved because of an internal client request.] Unfortunately they are rarely able to actually execute a big transaction. They do, however, have the power to say no. If they don't like you in terms of their risk assessment, they will say no. If there is a formal request for proposal (RFP) process, get to the protector early and win their trust in writing a favourable RFP. Use logic to sway them. Take them through it minute by minute and let them see how you have the best solution. Selling to the often highly analytical protector is not unlike pitching Mr Spock or Commander Data from Star Trek: this is not a popularity contest. Know the details, stick to the facts and be logical. If a ruler delegates to a protector, be sure to keep the ruler in the loop.

The Opposers. Don't like you for all the wrong reasons: they have a friend bidding for the contract; they are elitists; they are opposing the deal just because they CAN oppose the deal; or, they are feeling vindictive, emotionally opposed or prejudicial. Don't oppose the opposer. Recognize that they are being selfish. Deal with them by building stronger relationships with the people around them. Be so positive that the opposer has to either show a logical, business-based opposition to the deal, or they have to expose their emotional motivations. Always try to respect opposers for their stance, even to the point of complimenting them on their insights. Making peace with them is important because once the deal is done, they may be part of the ongoing relationship. Also, the last thing you need is for the opposer to make extra work or create a rift within the client company over you and your product.

The Contributors. Act as a second salesperson for you and allow behind-the-scenes entry to the decision maker. Contributors are often friends or the spouse of the ruler, or respected consultants, business associates or suppliers. They are often external players and there may be more than one. Build a network of contributors and use their access to the ruler to close a big deal. The effectiveness of your relationship with the contributors is a function of the history and credibility you already have with them. You haven't just met them. Often this second salesperson knows your work, knows your solution and has a history with you. That is what makes them credible on your behalf to the ruler. The more experience a contributor has with you and your solution, the easier it is to sell you.

Keep track of the Power Players, study them and build a strategy to strengthen your credibility and relationship with all of them.

Talking your way out of a deal

People tend to wait for their turn to talk, instead of listening. There are some good reasons – outside of the realm of biology and evolution – why we have two ears but only one mouth.

Bestselling author Zig Ziglar once said that he never saw a salesperson listen their way out of a deal, but he has seen many talk their way out of a deal. Although it is important to listen while face to face with a client to ensure that you really hear them and that they feel that you have heard them, it is also important to keep up a constant flow of communication with the client.

Watch out for dead air

Dead air between meetings and milestones can cool off a prospective client very quickly. Always have next steps in mind for client communication to keep them hot. Things like extra incentives and free newsletters can keep interest high, but be careful to avoid deluging a client with timewasters.

Breaking commitments

Making and keeping a commitment, even a small one before you close a deal, is a chance for you to demonstrate your ability to create results. It also gives the client an insight into your character, work ethic and the value that you have placed upon your relationship. Breaking commitments makes the client feel unvalued, uncomfortable and unsafe. We have all experienced personal relationships like that, which breed distrust and suspicion, and make people slow down or stop until they begin to feel safe with us again. This is an opportune time for a competitor to convert your client. Always meet your commitments.

Respect timelines

It is incumbent upon you to work yourself into your clients' business rhythm, not the other way around. If they tell you it will take six weeks to make a decision and yet you push for a decision, prematurely dangling discounts, special clauses or bonuses in front of them, you can run the risk of making them feel that you don't respect their timeline and are actually fitting THEM into your timeline and agenda. This could also cause them to wonder if you are perhaps desperate, maybe trying to meet your quota for the month without actually supplying a solution. This behaviour relegates you to the status of peddler, versus solution provider. One solution to this problem is to have plenty of clients in your sales pipeline so you are never desperate to close big deals.

Don't create work

Don't create work for your client or their team. If you offer a particularly innovative product or service, recognize and respect that your client will be dealing with change, even upheaval.

For example, if you are upgrading a computer network, make sure that downtime is minimized and that the new network or product can be adapted to by all users immediately and intuitively. If the client feels that this network will cause a major productivity dump and possibly leave many of the staff disoriented, they may choose another vendor or even stay with their old, out of date system.

Don't always sell the way the RFP is written

Sell yourself and your product legitimately, not the way the RFP is written or how the client would like you to sell to them. Ask yourself this: does my client understand my products as well as I do? Be assertive in requesting that additional issues be written into the RFP. Ask how the company is responding to risk.

KBI was once asked at the last minute to be the fifth company to tender a proposal for a sales training system to a group of senior executives at a large South African multinational company. The company forwarded the specifications they wanted. Bill Gibson decided to take a chance and, disregarding the specs that the proposal was supposed to follow, asked the executives whether they wanted a sales training system or improved sales results. They said they were after better results. Bill then gave them a 45-minute presentation on the processes and programs he used to produce major increases in sales at his existing clients over short periods of time. The client said Bill had uncovered exactly what they needed and come up with a plan that was simple, concise and to the point.

If Bill had been content to be relegated to the status of obedient order taker, he would have followed the RFP as given and not had a chance of actually closing the big deal. Instead, he took a risk, gained control, focused on results and delivered what the client was asking for, simply and without being slave to the RFP criteria.

Closing big deals is often about taking a leadership role and guiding your prospect to the best solution for them. Your client may not know how to find or evaluate the best solution. In the above case, the RFP was actually an obstacle to the client's success, which Bill helped them to recognize and overcome.

III.
The Closing Process from the First Contact

The Five Stages of Relationship Development

Is it plausible to expect someone to accept a marriage proposal on the second date? Of course not. But would-be big deal closers do this all the time in business, asking clients to commit to the business equivalent of marriage on the second date. Then they wonder why the client never calls back after the first few meetings.

Using the age-old theme of love as a parallel, we will now look at someone known by his colleagues as Flipper. He was on the continual quest for the perfect mate. A life partner no less. Since about age 28 (he's now 40) his relationships have lasted an average of four months. And all had the same theme: an extremely amorous first stage. He was a great catch: he had the great job, he had the great flat. Then at second stage, or exploration, he would go on several dates and they would begin to bond. He was good at connecting and developing harmony with others. At the development stage, going steady, things went very fast. He would spend all this time with them, friends forgotten. At month four, in utter shock, his potential partners found the relationship at an end. Most of them made the error of thinking that if it takes three months to get to the development stage, obviously it is only another month to commitment.

They, like many salespeople, made the wrong assumption and asked for too much business too soon, by asking for a long-term relationship.

A few years ago, a date of Flipper's sat down with me and expressed concern about the future of their relationship, she had a suspicion that the relationships' shelf life was only four months. I showed her a chart on the five stages of relationship development. I asked her, if it has taken three months to get to the development stage, how much longer she thought it would take to get to the commitment stage? She tentatively responded, "Another month or two?"

I said no way. Just because someone moves through stages one to three quickly, it doesn't mean they will get to stages four and five just as quickly. The majority of the relationships we all have are in the first three stages: attraction, exploration and development. We have relatively few in the last two stages: commitment and unity.

I told Flipper's girlfriend that most women he had been with hadn't understood the five stages of relationship development and had pressured him too quickly to commit: he just wasn't ready. From a business point of view, they tried to close the deal too quickly. Moving through the first three stages built a level of relationship momentum and optimistic impatience that would lead them to pressure him to pop the question. I told her to move slowly and identify his criteria for trust to move to the next step.

How many clients do you have that are like Flipper? We develop this high level of optimistic impatience as we feel the relationship momentum build. We get more orders, the client shares more information, and in our haste we forget to test where the relationship really is.

We jump in and try to close for a long-term commitment, exclusivity or a big retainer. But instead of closing, we watch the order book gradually dwindle, see less information being shared and watch the relationship stall.

The key is to always probe, test and evaluate to discern the kind of behaviour patterns and results the client expects us to display in order to qualify to move to the next level.

In any big deal, it is important to get an accurate read of what stage you are at with the client and the key power players in their network. Here's a quick look at the progression of a relationship from "hello" to "trusted advisor," or "I do":

Attraction stage. On a romantic level, this is flirtation; looking around for someone interesting. On a business level, a client is looking at what is unique about this person and is assessing their relative competence.

Exploration stage. The first few dates or meetings. This determines if the person qualifies for more time, energy and money, and if there is enough common ground to justify expending more effort with them. A client needs immediate, tangible results at this stage.

Development stage. The steady date stage. Trust begins here and real information is being shared. Exclusivity comes into play and enough information is known about each other to move on to the next stage. As a developing supplier, you are bonding here. This is the medium step, where a salesperson hasn't yet earned the long-term business but has earned the right to earn that business.

Commitment stage. Engaged and likely moving in together. The business relationship supersedes price. You are the supplier of choice, if not the sole supplier, and you are a tangible part of your client's long-term plans.

Unity stage. In a personal relationship, you would call this marriage. In business and in our personal lives, they need us as much as we need them. What we offer at this level is critical to their business success, and they are intent on retaining us as their supplier and trusted advisor.

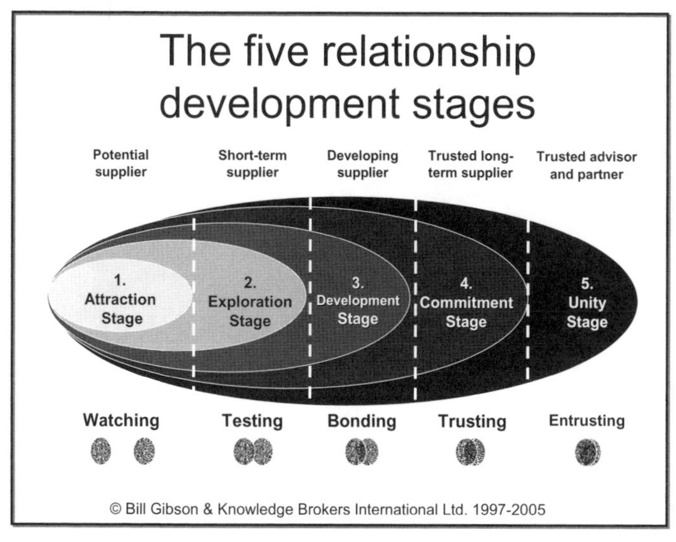

People tend to move through the various stages of relationship development at different speeds. Constantly test and evaluate. **Critical distinction:** It doesn't matter where *you* think the relationship is at, it's where the client thinks the relationship is at that dictates the level of commitment, trust and revenues!

Big deals only happen at the commitment and unity stage. Don't assume that you can force a close any earlier. Even if you do, you will still have to move through all five stages with your client in order to get the full buy-in to implement and sustain any big deal.

IV.
The Little Deal

Sometimes you have to close a little deal or a little client to get to the big deal or the big client. A small player may have a large conglomerate behind them composed of thousands of small players. My lawyer, Robert Palkowski, closed a deal a number of years ago with a businessman who was connected with some really big money. It became clear to Robert within two or three transactions that this gentleman didn't have his act together and was turning into a liability. Robert realized that this deal would unravel but he figured out that he could get access to the big money that was behind the scenes once the bigger players figured out the deal was going sideways. This unqualified businessman with little credibility had fluked his way into relationships with financial power brokers and would be on his way out soon, but not after he had served to gain access to big money for Robert.

Robert invested some time and effort in this deal that looked to be a waste of time, and within a few short weeks he was sitting at the table with the big players worth tens of millions of dollars.

We are not suggesting that you use people or manipulate behind their backs. If you end up in a situation with such an obvious downside, understand that you may still be able to capitalize on it by demonstrating your credibility and competence.

Before turning your nose up at the little deal, ask these questions: Is this person well networked in circles I am not that would benefit me? Does this person service big clients? If so, and I do business with him or her, is there potential to get referred to the big network?

How to recognize a small deal that will become a big deal

If a small order comes through, determine who is ordering and who is connected to that person. You may find that you have already moved into the exploration stage with a big client.

For example, I used to sell online ads. Often I had companies with ad budgets of $250,000 call me and give a $1,000 order, which lasts less than an hour on a high-traffic website. Literally a flash in the pan, these were the equivalent of a five-second advertisement spot run once on primetime television. Producing measurable results under these circumstances was, to say the least, difficult.

These companies weren't running around placing 250 orders for $1,000. Rather, they were looking for someone who could prove that they were worthy of winning a million dollars or more in advertising spending. They were testing for uniqueness, ability to execute, quickness of response and creativity. They were saying, "give us a reason to do big business with you."

We may never get the million-dollar client if we make the $1,000 order a low priority. Treat the little guy and the little order with respect. Take the time to analyze and probe, and seek out spin-off opportunities.

V.
The All-important Follow-up and Follow-through

As discussed earlier, frequency is the key to converting competitors' clients. As the "Sales Conversion Ratio" chart showed, your first contact will convert only 2% of that business on average. Second contact yields only 3% and onwards until the fourth contact, which will pull 10% of the business. But it is only on the fifth contact and onwards that 81% of all conversion business occurs. The reality is that you may have to contact the client 25 times to close the big deal but you have to get used to making at least five contacts.

The key factor is to avoid harassment, and the cardinal rule of contact is to never initiate contact unless you have figured out how to add real value to the client that will build credibility.

Frequency breeds trust. Remember the maxim that says after three good meetings, a client will generally trust you 70% more than at the first meeting.

A 1995 study of sales in the dry goods industry showed that only 12% of the salespeople in the industry continued contacting the client after two solid rejections. But that small percentage that was willing to weather three or more rejections made 80% of all commissions paid in the entire industry.

Here is an anecdotal lesson in frequency:

One Friday, a salesman named Glen bounded in the door of my office. A bigger-than-life happy guy with a good smile and a relaxed, confident demeanor, Glen said he was sorry to drop in uninvited, but he had been in a meeting with the businessman next door and had been referred by him to me.

Jack next door actually popped in to introduce Glen in person, saying he had sent him down to say hello. Glen sold document-management services. I said I wasn't buying, didn't want to waste Glen's time and blew him off. Glen left some brochures and arranged to pop in the next week. I frankly didn't want them and didn't read them.

Glen came back and offered to buy a coffee or lunch. On the way to coffee we made small talk, and Glen gradually became likeable. Later that day, Glen faxed me a "good to have met you" note. The next Friday, Glen came back with two coffees, one for me. I invited him in for a chat and we talked business a bit but I still wasn't interested in buying anything.

The next week, Glen didn't come at all, but my company had a fax crisis in the middle of a big project for big money. Glen showed up in the nick of time with a demo fax that he loaned to me. He saved the day. A week later, Glen sold me on a document-management system worth several thousand dollars.

Throughout, Glen politely and with a good dose of humour refused to take no for an answer. His style and ability to entertain and add value to my day kept me receptive and open to communicating with him, and kept my door open. Glen refused to be average and kept going after the fifth no. He followed up and followed through. Constantly. Even after it looked like he had lost.

The frequency toolkit

I can see you doing the math. You are asking the question: "If it will take me four to twelve contacts over, say, six months, to close big deals, how do I do this without harassing the client and inviting a restraining order?"

The key is to never make contact without adding value to that client's day.

Never.

The more value you add, the more receptive they are and the more time you get each subsequent time you make contact.

When you ask that age-old question over the telephone, "is this a good time?" even a busy executive will say, "sure I have a couple of minutes."

There are almost as many ways to contact a prospective client as there are reasons to get in touch, but you need more reasons to chat than to ask, "you ready to buy yet?"

You can call them because you are referring business to them. You can follow up from an e-mail to be sure they can open an attachment. You can have a senior executive, assistant or a technical representative call on another issue. You can make a conference call to introduce a new team member. Say happy birthday. Happy New Year. Merry Christmas. Call to offer congratulations if you read a great press release featuring your client. Do a needs analysis update or confirmation. Invite them to a function. Give them information on a competitor. Call to do a customer service audit. Tell them about an upcoming conference or seminar they might be interested in. Call their attention to a relevant business article. Call as a follow-up to a courier package delivery, etc.

Bear in mind that not all people respond to all mediums the same way. Some executives work solely by e-mail right up until it is time to close a deal. Others really need face to face communication while some are perfectly content to close deals over the phone.

We can maximize our frequency selling approach using multiple mediums of contact. What we achieve from this is a greater share of mind than our competitors and the ability to have the client see us, experience us and hear from us in multiple value-added ways.

These are the contact tools that have to be in any salesperson's frequency toolkit:

VI.
Nick Usborne on e-mail

With senior executives, e-mails must be brief (unless they've asked for a proposal), they must be personalized and they must be recognizable. Make sure there is an obvious benefit statement in the message and don't insult senior executives by trying to sell them with an e-mail. Keep it in the realm of contact only. If you must send an attachment, use the PDF format, as most people won't open anything but a PDF to ensure that messages are virus-free.

To gather greater insight on e-mail as a tool for communicating with decision makers, we spoke to Internet-writing expert Nick Usborne. Nick (www.nickusborne.com) is an expert on writing for the web and has advised Yahoo!, MSN, Intuit, Getty Trust and Wells Fargo, to name just a few.

Now, over to Nick:

"When it comes to C-level [chief executive level, as in CEO, CFO] executives, there is one thing in particular to keep in mind: they are smart and busy enough not to get bogged down in 'discovery'. That is to say, if a decision is going to be made about, say, working with a new supplier, the executive will likely have a number of people beneath and around him or her who will do a lot of the donkey-work.

If you do manage to reach the C-level by e-mail or get him or her to your site, make an executive summary available to them quickly and simply. In other words, don't expect a busy person to browse through your site, putting all the relevant information together. Instead, make a PDF file, or whatever, available for download from your home page or direct from an e-mail or newsletter. Enable your prospect to download and print the document and read it at a time that suits them best.

Target the people around and beneath the C-level executive. It's their job to put together the information that exec needs. Give them what they need in the form in which they need it. This usually comprises summaries of core information. Again, present a PDF option so they can download and print the information. These people are busy too, so the closer you come to giving them the information they need in the format they need to present it upwards, the more they will like you. In addition to PDFs, make a "printable version" of each summary page available.

If you do manage to get a C-level executive on your opt-in e-mail list, and the e-mails are being opened, be sure that you deliver tangible value with every e-mail. Keep the messages brief, get directly to the point. Personalize the e-mail with the executive's name. Include your full name and complete contact information every time. In other words, have the e-mails come from a particular individual...never from 'The Widget Inc Sales Team'. Build a reputation over time for delivering valuable information.

MOST IMPORTANT OF ALL:

Do your homework before targeting C-level executives. Don't put together a program that is designed to be all things to all people. Create separate programs to focus tightly on the particular needs of niches within particular industries. In other words, make the content of your e-mails and newsletters compellingly relevant."

Faxes

E-mail has become so ubiquitous that the fax has almost become a novelty, and remains quite rare in the average business day. Putting pen to paper and faxing it produces a hard copy at the other end that sits on someone's desk and forces them to do something with it. The recipient can hoist aboard all the information in a glance and not have to scroll down as they would have to do with an e-mail.

A couple of years ago, I sent this fax (below) to a client. I wasn't getting the results I wanted using phone calls and e-mails. Admittedly this idea wasn't an original; at KBI we've been encouraging clients to do this for years so I thought I'd try out my own advice with this hard to reach client. Here's what I faxed him:

Fax From the Desk of Shane Gibson

Subject: Mr. John Doe, We Urgently Need to Connect!

Dear John,

As you know I've called you to talk about setting the dates for the country wide training program we were planning on doing in the New Year. I have also e-mailed you at least another four times. I'm sure you're busy like most people today so I don't want you to call me or e-mail me back; just simply check the appropriate box and fax it back to me.

❐ Shane please call me at __________ pm/am on ___________ to set the dates.

❐ Shane I'm really busy right now and would like you to follow-up with me next month.

❐ Shane we've decided not to use your services right now.

❐ Shane lose my number and e-mail and never contact me again!

Two minutes later, I got a fax back saying "GO TO HELL" in all capitals. My heart leaped into my throat and my heart rate went through the roof. Then my phone rang. It was that client, chuckling away. He said there was a dozen people like me trying to get a hold of him and he was getting a hundred e-mails a day. He appreciated the innovative approach to making contact and had himself a good chuckle in the process. And I got the business.

VIP functions

Take a client to a sports event, host a dinner with clients, or take clients to a conference. Make these activities distinctive and exclusive enough that your client knows they are on your A-list.

Coffees, lunches and dinners

Simply put, mankind was made to break bread together.

Ethical gifts

These should be unique and thoughtful but not overboard so as to look like you are trying to buy the clients' business. A book on the industry. A moderately priced piece of art. An in-kind contribution. All of these work.

Calls from your team

A call from one of your senior executives to thank a client for the business keeps the client connected to your company, as well as shows them that your whole company is supportive. Also, have your tech staff call their tech staff to talk business. This is a layered frequency tool. All the major people in your hierarchy call the client, who feels the red carpet being rolled out for them and gets a sense of being connected to a true support team.

Christmas gifts

Be unique without being funny. Maybe have some good wine made, get a well-designed label done up with your company's brand and send it to clients.

Time plus genuine sincere assistance builds a strong relationship. From there, commitment is natural.

The frequency toolkit is specific to big deals alone. Frequency is a powerful tool but it is also an expensive endeavour. If you triple your frequency to an unprofitable prospect, they don't become profitable or bigger. They just become three times more costly. With marginal clients, find other ways to make contact by means of automated systems, like an electronic newsletter or standardized cards in regular, large mailouts.

The key here is to maximize value, frequency and the variety of contact mediums you use.

Most of Knowledge Brokers International's clients that have implemented the frequency toolkit approach have used a simple system for tracking client contacts. It fits on one sheet of paper. The name of one of your most wanted clients goes on the top left of the sheet and down the side you list the frequency tools you are going to use with the client and the number of times you will be using that tool that year.

The next step is to set up a way to remind yourself to contact the client frequently, using your scheduler, a computer program or a monthly calendar. Below is a sample frequency tracking sheet. For each key account prospect you can set specific frequency goals with a variety of tools. The benefit of this format is that it gives you a sample at-a-glance look at your present level of contact and what needs to happen in the future:

Client Name: ____

Contact Name: ____________________________ Date: ___________

Tools and Activities	Frequency / Number of Tools intended to use	Target Dates Completed
Phone calls	12	December 15th January 7th
One on one meeting	4	
Technical Teleconference	1	November 13th
Meeting or Teleconference	1	October 22nd
E-mail	15	September 4th, October 4th, December 11th
Thank-you cards	2	October 22nd
Lunch / coffee	2	
Greeting / promotional card	1	
Articles	2	
Send quotes and references	1	
Send a referral	1	
Send a personal fax	3	
Letters	2	
VIP function	1	December 12th
Invite to seminar	1	
Wine and cheese at the office	1	January 8th
Notes, Goals and Steps for the next 12 months:		

The University of Victoria's Co-operative Education Program took this process to the next level and integrated a system called Mamook into their customer relationship management strategy. When program coordinators target a potential corporate partner and enter them in the system, Mamook reminds them on a regular basis which tools and mediums to use with each client. This has automated the entire process for them, ensures that there are no gaps in the communications process and allows entire teams to have the same view of a large partner like the federal government.

VII.
Needs Analysis Selling

A number of years ago, Bill Gibson worked at CJCH / C100 FM Radio in Halifax which is part of the CHUM Group, and was billed as one of Canada's top radio advertising salesmen. He got so good that the then-named Radio Bureau of Canada toured him across the country to talk about his approach to selling radio airtime using the needs analysis approach.

Bill developed a client-marketing questionnaire that delved well beyond what most ad salesmen did. This caused him to be seen as a peer to the clients he was selling to, and a provider of solutions and resources. Bill never sold; he always listened. He would often recommend print ads or training programs to clients instead of radio ads. This built his credibility. Clients would often call after he had sold ads to them, to ask about what to do in particular business situations.

With his questionnaire, Bill was developing a template for needs analysis. He simply became more knowledgeable than his competitors and peers, and reaped the rewards.

A needs analysis serves as an in-depth record that can be very useful for all levels of sales and implementation within your organization. It also serves as a corporate record and reference tool, allowing sales and tech staff to work from the same information.

More importantly, a needs analysis raises the salesperson to the level of peer from that of simply product-peddler, conferring a street-level MBA. You gain knowledge and insight you didn't know you needed. You speak the language of your client, you sound like your client, you have felt their pain and you know the challenges they face. That credibility is hard to compete with.

If asked correctly, most of the vital information to be gained from a prospective client may come from only 20% of the core questions. The other 80% isn't throwaway though. It serves as a way to connect and build rapport.

The process starts with easy questions such as, "where would you like to see your company going in 18 months." It moves on to more focused queries on budgets, challenges and goals.

Open questions build rapport and elicit information that we didn't necessarily know we needed. For example, "Why go to tender on this contract instead of using the present provider?"

Closed questions are just looking for a yes or no, and that is usually what you get.

Directive questions lead your client to reflect on a topic that you want them thinking about. For example, in leading an insurance client to think about director liability you may ask "...based on the current market, with more CEO's being investigated for malfeasance, what are your thoughts on reducing that risk?"

The needs analysis should flow like a natural process. Watch Larry King on CNN to learn how to ask questions. King asks open, pace setting questions, then at the end, after what seems like little prompting, he ends up with information that no one expected him to get, particularly the person being interviewed.

Effective interviewing requires a variety of questions to keep you and the listener interested and engaged in the process. If the needs analysis is too open and general, the conversation floats and reveals little of substance. If it is too closed, the listener slips into a trance and the process becomes an interrogation. If done well, there will be a natural flow to the end of the needs analysis.

Once you are near the end of the needs analysis, try a test question along the lines of "...Do you think we have missed anything that might be pertinent to writing a proposal?" Or signal the end by saying, "...Last thing: any questions for me?"

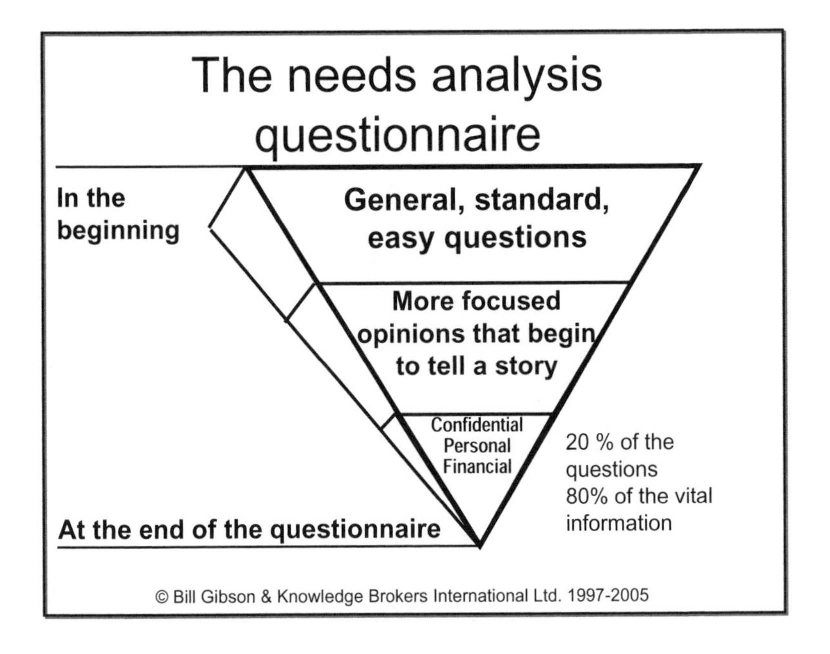

At this point you will be able to evaluate the signals you receive from your client, based on the confidence created by the needs analysis, and you can assess the distance you have covered towards closing the deal. Now is the time to look for buying signals from them, such as questions about the price or your product, or the projected rollout or scope, or what kind of agreement is necessary to move forward.

At the end of the needs analysis, you will have a higher level of trust and rapport with the client, so even a general, open-ended question will yield genuine, confidential information that wouldn't have been divulged at the start of the session. And, don't just switch off at this point. If the client wants to keep talking and even socialize now, this very social conversation can garner confidential and important business intelligence for you.

Following is a sample needs analysis that might be used by a leadership consulting firm in an initial meeting with a prospective client:

Leadership Consulting Client Needs Analysis

1) Add in personal details, name address, phone number etc.

2) I like to get a good idea of where an organization is heading. It allows me to ensure that anything I might suggest we can do for you is in line with your business goals and vision. Where do you see your organization heading in the next 18 months?

3) What do you see as some of your biggest challenges you'll face during this period of time?

4) What do you see as your biggest opportunities?

5) Have you invested in consulting of this nature for your organization before?

6) What does your organizational structure look like?

7) Where are your strong leaders and producers?

8) What makes them strong?

9) Where are your bottlenecks and weaker links?

10) What causes these challenges?

11) What major changes have you initiated and/or anticipated?

12) What resistance or challenges have you encountered during the change or in anticipation to this change?

13) As you see coaching and training as a tool to take your team to the next level, where would you see the applications?

14) In order for a program like this to be successful what would have to be achieved and by when?

15) How do you typically budget for a program like this? Is it on a per person basis or a percentage of revenues, for example?

16) List the areas of challenge or desired growth and improvement and then rate them 1-12 (with 1 being most important to address now and 12 being merely convenient to address).

1) ______________________________

2) ______________________________

3) ______________________________

4) ______________________________

5) ______________________________

6) ______________________________

7) ______________________________

8) ______________________________

9) ______________________________

10) ______________________________

11) ______________________________

12) ______________________________

The value of questions and the subconscious

The value of questions is all in the asking. Contemporary psychology research shows that about 7% of a question's effectiveness depends on the actual words used, 23% is tone of voice, while facial gestures and body language are each responsible for a full 35% of the effectiveness of a question, and for the level of rapport established and maintained.

Psychologists say that the conscious mind can retain about seven distinct chunks of information at any given time without some of that information slipping into the realm of the subconscious or drifting away on the ether. Yet, at this moment, your subconscious is monitoring millions of bits of data.

Recall a time when you have walked into a room and met someone who caused a negative reaction or impression in you. That was your subconscious becoming aware of a level of incongruity or lack of rapport with that person. At that time, if you could have stepped outside of yourself and observed yourself watching this person, you would have noted that that person's communication traits are very different from your own. Your subconscious is saying that this person is different; this person is unfamiliar; this person may not be safe.

Both consciously and unconsciously, we like to do business with people like us. Observing another's body language, eye movements, gestures and tonality, and shifting our communications to be more similar to theirs creates a level of subconscious rapport. The subconscious says, "this person is familiar, this person is like me, this person is probably safe."

In sales, it is often the salesperson who creates the doubt. The client generally wants to develop a rapport, hoping you are the one with the product or service they want. They want to get the buying process over with and get on with their agenda.

And again, once the needs analysis is done, if the deal isn't ready to be closed then and there, always be sure to have a commitment for the next step. Avoid letting too much time pass between the needs analysis, when your level of mind-share with the client is on top, and the next step. Over time, the client gets busy with the day-to-days of the job, your competitors call and a million other details crowd their day. And your mind-share erodes.

Don't be afraid to suggest the next step to your client because they might not actually know what the next step is, but don't want to admit it. The next step could be a trial run, a meeting with the CFO to go over line items in a proposal or even starting phase one of a five-phase proposal. At the very least this will preempt a nagging round of phone tag and allow you to keep the information fresh. You can also maintain a high level of urgency in your client to read any material you might have left with them.

VIII.
Team Selling

"One is too few a number to achieve greatness"

The above quote is from John Maxwell, a bestselling author of leadership books. In sales and business a champion is always backed by a network and support system. Even entrepreneurs have networks.

In most corporate relationships the key account executive brings a team with them, and they sell as a team.

The key factor is to make sure everyone is up to date on all aspects of the client and the deal. Invariably, some members of the team end up having more information than others. If the client questions a team member and they get caught out as lacking key information, credibility can be immediately lost and team cohesiveness can suffer due to a loss of confidence in a team member.

All team members must know the core objections that a client may have to the proposed solution or product. Similarly, they have to be briefed on all information that is being disclosed to your team by the client.

Early in my career, I was working in a three-person team on a pitch to a high-tech firm. The team leader stepped up and went hard into the pitch in the boardroom, but didn't introduce my colleague or myself. We won the business but the team leader then left the country and appointed me as the key account executive. The client knew nothing about us and perceived us as a couple of lackeys sitting on a log watching the boss, then waiting for him to come back to town.

To keep this from reoccurring with future clients, my colleague and I built an "edification strategy": we each sat down and wrote a personal pitch on our experiences, strengths and knowledge base. We gave this to the team leader for him to present to clients. That built our credibility. Even though the boss was generally the rainmaker on most deals, he couldn't close and service clients on his own so he tactfully talked about my colleague and I as his teammates, highlighting our strong points and the value we brought to the team.

In these situations, teammates can say things about you that you can't say for yourself. You can boast about your teammates and thereby raise everyone's profile. Why not? Hockey players do it all the time. On your own it could look like bragging but in a team context it contributes to an impression of a confident, tightly knit group of professionals.

To avoid decision vacuums, a team leader must be chosen. The leader reserves the right to cut teammates off, make decisions on the fly and appeal to the needs of the client in the moment. The team leader then begins to coordinate communications and contacts. The leader is the knowledge manager. They deal with the entire power player network on the client side. They facilitate internal team meetings as well as full-team meetings with the client, in order to meet and assess the key players on the client side to make the most of opportunities...as well as opposition.

Keep the team cohesive. As much as possible, the whole team should go through all the stages of client relationship development. Try to keep all the players consistent and keep job rotation to a minimum, as you are selling the team to your client.

Communications and lateral thinking are critical. You might be selling to a company with multiple divisions, like a commercial bank. With various levels of your company possibly selling to the same client, step back and begin to form a concept of team sales and servicing. Coordinate and identify opportunities, and identify a team leader who will be responsible for leading and collaborating the team sale for that client. Look for the member of your organization who has the best network and relationship with that client because they will be better at identifying opportunities. Tracking should be rigourous. Have a process in place that enables you to monitor your progress at each point of contact through internal focus meetings.

Team account planning

A profile of the client should include a Strengths, Weaknesses, Opportunities, Threats (SWOT) analysis looking at the client's position in the marketplace.

The profile should also include discussion of the goals, leadership, competitors, state of their industry, shifts in the consumer market and a workup of their ideal client.

To get this information, scan newspapers and magazines in the general and industry press, subscribe to the client's newsletter and do regular searches on the Internet. More informally, do your networking where employees of the client firm are likely to gather. Spending time with the front-line people will definitely give you a perspective on your client's pains. Former employees are also good for unvarnished opinions. A service provider to the client who isn't a competitor is also an excellent source of tactical intelligence. If you sell roofing materials to the housing market, partnering with a flooring company to get information on general contractors is a smart move. These cross-discipline relationships are rarely unrewarding.

Key components needed in a team account plan

Yes. Closing big deals is about the relationship. That said, the difference between any deal and a big deal is the level of organization you need to maintain credibility in the relationship. A great deal can unravel when a series of seemingly minor promises and details go awry. When you throw a team of players into the sales arena, the chance of error increases drastically. Having a team account plan to manage commitments and knowledge is vital to holding it all together. The account plan can be broken down into the following five key components:

Information Analysis Chart

The purpose is to summarize key client pains, connect them with a solution you can provide and produce a benefit statement that the client will buy. Condense your needs analysis data into a more usable format in chart form (see below).

Power player network snapshot

This snapshot outlines key needs, desires and issues with your top power players, allowing the team to plan an approach with a high level of awareness and multiple perspectives (see below).

Conflict or cross-over grid

As discussed earlier, in a team-selling environment there are often multiple divisions selling complementary offerings to the same buyer or buying groups. In order to reduce redundancy and increase collaboration it is important to note where two or more people in your company may be contacting the buyer or buyers and coordinate a seamless, collaborative team approach (see below).

Team storyboard action flowchart

This provides an at a glance flowchart of the entire team's activities with the client, allowing teammates to maintain accountability, momentum and direction in a complex sale (see below).

List of frequency selling tools to be used by the team

As we discussed previously in the section of frequency tools, listing and planning key value-added contacts that you will make as a team will ensure a higher level of organization, consistency of message and will maximize the use of all methods and mediums of contact.

Information Analysis Chart

Information gathered	How can we help.	Benefit to the client	Who provides the solution?
Challenges forecasting revenues from new markets (no history)	Introduce client to our CRM partner and provide them with pipeline management software and Knowledge Brokers International Profit Builder Process.	Better tracking on progression data and trending from all reps in real time. They get a time-proven process they can count on for accurate forecasting.	Shane and Marius in partnership with SA CRM Inc.
Too many small clients eating up key account manager's time	Implement targeting module and help client structure a small business team (inside sales) to deal with smaller accounts.	Key account outside salespeople will be focused on high ROI clients (big revenue clients). Smaller clients will get better service = better branding and goodwill.	Bill and Marius
Staff are typically failing to implement what they learn at sales training programs	Provide a series of implementation sheets, templates and sales coaching training for management.	Quicker and higher return on investment on training. More focused and efficient meetings between sales management and staff.	Shane and Bob
No HR Process or system for sales team.	Provide templates, instruction, hiring techniques and guidelines to client. Create a training and development plan.	Reduced liability, higher productivity. Ready for future expansion.	Denis and Shane

Here you isolate the one, the true, the burning need for them to do business with you. Be careful to keep a clear focus and to avoid gathering so much information that you forget the reason you are gathering data.

Charting the power players

The power player network chart lists the core information you already have on the client and hence will show what is still needed. It will break out the development stage of the relationship and determine what you need to do to take it to the unity stage. This chart can of course be used by individual big deal closers as well as by teams.

Power Player Network

Power Player ID	**Who?**	**Notes, Concerns, Opportunities**
Ruler	John Smith	After the needs analysis, John seemed to be open and comfortable with all three team members (Malcolm, Denis and Shane) who did the interview. He's committed to do what it takes but needs reassurance that the executive will remain harmonious and costs won't get out of hand.
Users	Alisa Jao and Fred Green seem to be the two most vital users to engage.	Let's ensure that both of these people feel involved, valued and recognized. Also spend some time with them understanding what process they presently use.
Protector	Alisa Jao (CFO) Paul McCarthy (VP Sales)	Alisa sees the "big cheques" going out to external consultants, she needs to be kept in the loop and communicated with continually to keep her onside with the process. She can also give us insight into other financial drains that aren't evident on the balance sheet. Paul McCarthy is very cautious about how this may

		impact his team and short-term sales productivity – it is important for us to get his feedback and communicate challenges immediately.
Contributor	Bob Koch, Management Consultant Mike Comeau, VP Jett Marketing and golfing buddy of John Smith	Both of these people have John Smith's ear and trust. We need to keep these people updated on the project and process of closing this deal. They may be helpful.
Opposer	Paul Smith (VP Marketing)	Even after our initial information gathering meeting, Paul seemed to oppose the process. We need to meet with him, get feedback, involve him and let him know we value his input in the process.
Navigator	Bob Koch and Bob Worth	Bob Koch as a management consultant can help navigate us through some of the political dynamics and unofficial influencers; his knowledge is based upon a one-year-old relationship. Bob Worth, who formerly worked for the company, will be able to give us other insight into the key power players and their politics.

Conflict / Crossover Matrix

Create a grid of all the key players on your team and the client's team. Detail who deals with whom, and who will coordinate on your team. If two of your people are dealing with the same person on the client side, make sure they develop a plan to collaboratively service the client, share information and cross-sell and promote.

Conflict / Crossover Matrix					
Contacts	**Marius**	**Shane**	**Denis**	**Bill**	**Bob**
John Smith	x	x	x	x	x
Alisa Jao	x				x
Fred Smith		x	x		x
Paul McCarthy		x			x
Fred Green				x	
Bob Koch	x				
Mike Comeau	x				
Bob Worth		x			

Working in a team-lead situation allows the advantage of educating each member of the team on what their colleagues bring to the table. It also identifies cross-selling opportunities, affords flexibility and gets each team member closer to being solution-focused. A team-lead perspective allows the team to get a detailed perspective on the whole client.

The Storyboard Action Plan

At KBI, we use a storyboard action system to map out sales and marketing plans. The following page shows a simplified one-page plan.

I like this format because I can tell at a glance what the next steps are in the sales process and where I need to focus my energy as the sales team lead.

Topic:

Project: Big Bank sales e-learning program

Storyboard Action System™

Date: Feb. 5, 2005

Project Leader: Mike

Team Member	Week 1	Week 2	Week 3	Week 4	Week 5	Week 6	Notes
Mike (Key Account Manager)	Do an overall needs analysis with Banks e-training academy team and VP of Sales	Share findings with whole team, book an initial presentation time with Big Bank	Send meeting agenda to Big Bank and internal team. Make sure the team is on schedule	Confirm meeting times and attendees. Prep team and do the pitch.	Present revised plan to Big Bank and get contract for phase 1 signed		
Sarah (Chief Technology Officer)	Look at similar past clients and what tech resources will be needed for a project	Have a project timeline ready for team and rough costing	Meet with Eddie, Bill, and LMS co ensure things are running smoothly for Demo	Present project timeline to client		Meet with Big Bank tech team to talk about security and servers	
Eddie (Instructional Designer)	Pull together most recent training programs and give to Eddie	Begin to break down modules into effective e-learning format for demo	Finish re-purposing training content and get it onto the LMS servers for test run with Bill.	Be by the one and prepped in case sales team needs support during pre-sentations		Begin re-purposing the rest of the content	
Bill (Author and Trainers)	Quote on a license for 500 people to use the Learning Management System	Review Mike's needs analysis findings and adapt content for training program demo	Call Big Bank VP to say hello and connect before next week. Meet with Eddie re Demo.	Be by the phone and prepped in case sales team needs support during presentations		Customize content for this Bank	
Whole Team		Meet and collaborate on solution, costing, client needs, and plan pitch	Run Demo. Meet for dry run on presentation, share new information, role-play scenarios	Meet after client presentation to adjust based upon feedback.	Meet to plan for Phase 1 – and celebrate!	Meet and review project milestones and share up-sell potential opps.	
Palkowski & Company Law Co	Draft agreements for Bank and our LMS Partner	Provide rough draft of agree-ment based scope of project	Adjust contract with changes in scope.	Make changes needed in contract and payment schedule.	Give final approval to contract. Set up trust acct.		

IX.
Big Deal Closers are Big Communicators

I am on author John Maxwell's CD of the month club. He speaks about the difference between educators, indoctrinators and communicators. Educators and indoctrinators can tend to take simple things and make them complicated. They create labels, use jargon and make comprehension more difficult. On the other hand, communicators can take the complex and render it simple.

A large component of communication is getting in synch with the prospect. As we know, selling is not just facts and data, but it is about creating an environment where an act of faith can take place, built on trust, which is driven by credibility. To delve deeper, credibility is built on a value set. From a sales perspective, when a big deal closer takes complex ideas and simplifies them, they appeal to their clients' value set.

There is no ideal personality style for selling. As with other factors, it is based on the flexibility to adapt one's style to the clients' style. A good rule of thumb: People wish to be communicated to in the same way they themselves communicate.

Take a moment to plot yourself on the following chart. Rate from 0 to 10, with 0 being unstructured, 10 being structured. A quick thought on this rating. If you are 0, people will probably have to climb over the empty pop cans and old newspapers in your car. And there are probably moldy cups in your sink as we speak. If you are a 10, people probably walk into your house and wonder, "is this a museum or does someone actually live here?"

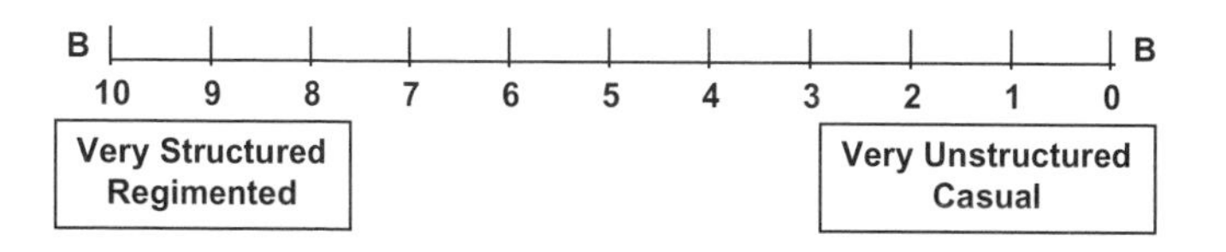

Then rate yourself from 0-10, with 0 being quiet and 10 being outspoken.

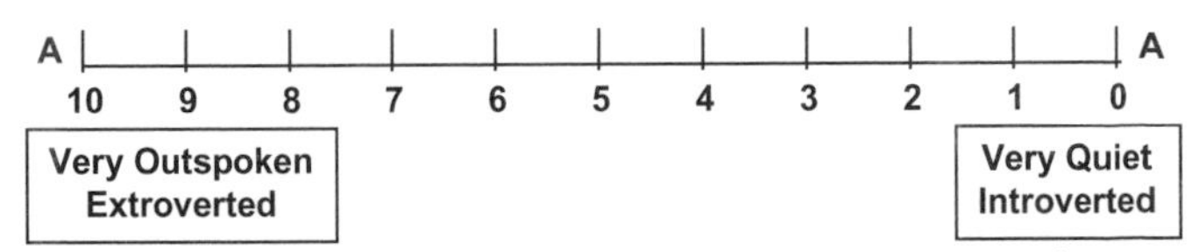

Once you have plotted this, intersect your two plots in the quadrant as in the diagram below:

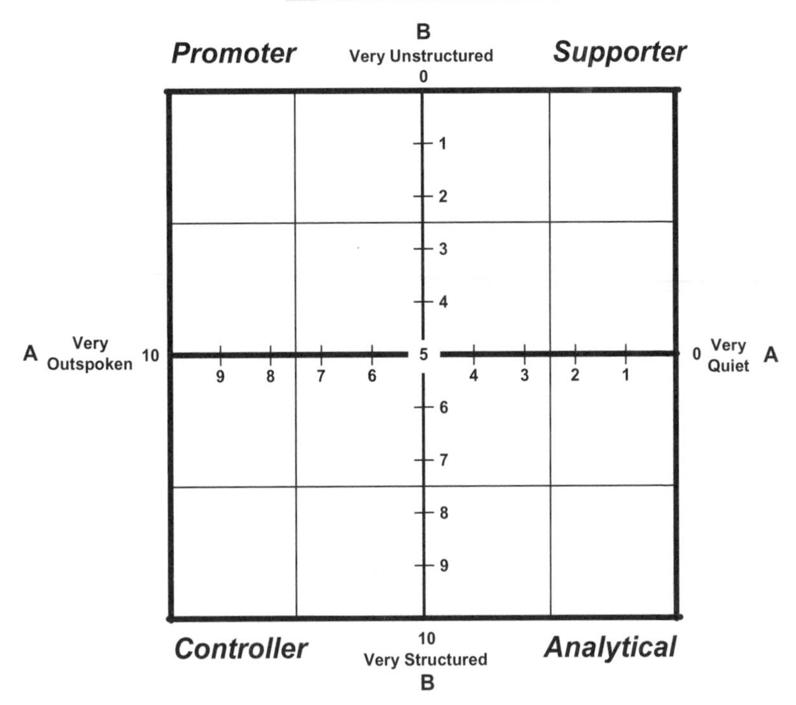

The four personality styles

The Supporter is generally disorganized or unstructured and is sensitive, but their strength is their ability to be highly aware. The supporter is great as part of team because they seem to know how everyone is doing. They are the caretaker. The downside is they are easily hurt and take everything personally. They lack structure. Timings and budgets are suggestions for supporters; not really tangible, so therefore appeals to the bottom line fall on deaf ears with supporters.

Round numbers off for a supporter and be aware that relationships are number one for them. They will buy from you to gain approval or to support another person. They love to help others but need guarantees and assurances. Show them how risk is handled and how nobody gets hurt.

If you are selling to them, adapting to meet their style involves slowing down, being sincere, being aware of eye contact and talking about your feelings. Be sure to respect their space, ask them for support, show trust in them and indicate that you are trustworthy. Don't box them in. Be real and comfortable. Take the time to understand them on a personal level. Personal matters hold great credibility for the supporter. Loved ones and friends are their lives. Don't take risks. Invest significant time in the relationship before you try to close the deal. If they trust you they are likely to make a decision based on minimal facts.

Unlike the supporter, *the Analytical* is the most likely personality type to be prejudiced against the stereotypical salesperson. A typical salesperson in their eyes lacks substance, is overbearing and loud, and may even drive a red convertible. Analyticals are highly attuned to insincerity. They are very organized but not expressive and verbal but not animated. The promoter would think that for an analytical to go to parties, they have to rent a personality. They value specifics, facts and data. Their big thing is to save face. They hate to be seen as wrong or to lose credibility. They never forget it if you put them on the spot publicly and will get you back. Long after you have forgotten about the situation, they are still plotting your demise. Analyticals tend to lack spontaneity.

I once worked with a guy who was so analytical that he resembled Commander Data on Star Trek. One day I walked into his office when he was away and saw his daytimer on his desk. I asked my colleague if we should look into it. She said not to touch it, as he would know. It was a risk I was willing to take though. I carefully negotiated my way past his lined-up pencils and squared-off piles of immaculate paper, and opened the daytimer to that day's date. There in bold letters was written, "Spontaneous day. Take out $80 and do what I want." He was so analytical that he actually planned his spontaneity. Years later, he has actually become a strong business associate of mine. His skills are a strong complement to my sort of loose, unstructured approach. He and I had to do a lot of adaptation of our styles to work together effectively. He had to loosen up and I had to provide some sustained substance.

So remember the watchword for the analytical is thoroughness. Be aware that if you pass along a huge report, they will read everything. Everything. Time – and your deal – will stop until they have read, digested and fully understand every scrap of material sent their way.

Be sensitive to their thinking. Their specialty is accuracy. They are the logistics head, chief of procurement or the key scientist. Analyticals tend to gravitate toward teaching, the law, medicine and engineering. They can take a long time to make a decision. In a crisis, they lock the door and plan their way out.

Avoid any action until the analytical has had a chance to plan. If you put too much pressure on them, they will avoid calls. When selling, cover the fine points, be specific, do your research, be accurate, deliver quality information and don't be afraid to use charts, graphs and whatever else brings your point home. Ask for their input, because they are proud of their powers of logic, but don't be pushy or flashy or get too close.

Be friendly but don't overstep any boundaries. When they are talking, don't interrupt them and have a healthy respect for their schedule – because they always follow their schedule. Quick ways to lose credibility include not knowing the facts and not offering linear, logical options. Personal feelings and the big picture do not compute and are not important to the analytical.

The Controller loves results. Action is all that matters, and talk is cheap. They are good decision makers and can assess a situation quickly and take action. They double their efforts under crisis and like to save time. They like to be in charge. Having control, or at least the appearance of control, is a major value for them. Don't sell to them in the traditional sense. Rather, provide options and let them pick. Ask for feedback on what they think is the best option. Lay out probabilities, not definites. Show support to their conclusions. Their specialty is "action now."

Controllers are doers, so they can tend towards insensitivity and they need to be right even when they are wrong. They think arguing is a sport and can get autocratic under pressure: the "my way or the highway" school of thought.

If you are selling to a controller, show up early and finish early to gain credibility. Keep profits in mind, be precise, be clean and don't waste time. Talk about the bottom line. Stick to business, don't get personal, and don't be chatty. Hit the highlights and remember not to argue with them. Maintain a strong physical posture and tonality. Just be aware not to challenge them in any way.

The two personalities found dead in crosswalks most often are the analytical and the controller. The analytical can be in the middle of a crosswalk and see a big truck bearing down but be unable to gather enough facts and data to make a decision and would get run over. A controller would see the truck, step into the crosswalk and think "I have a right to cross this road." And continue that argument with the truck for about a split second.

The Promoter loves applause. Even if you are faking it they don't care. They make for the best starters but they don't finish so well. The promoter is all about economizing on effort. Listen for them to ask how to get things done with little effort, or how to get credit for themselves and get someone else to do it, or how to not do it but still get the credit. They are big-picture oriented, and pay attention to dreams and intuitions. Promoters are influenced by testimonials and incentives and like to keep up with the Joneses. They are expressive, like to build rapport and can fit well into any environment; promoters are chameleons. Their big thing is recognition, so you have to sugarcoat criticism.

Their downfalls include not finishing tasks, thinking out loud and a lack of focus. Their backup style under pressure is to attack by shifting blame.

Once you understand that the promoter is all about fun, big picture, being first and being best, then they become easy to sell to. When selling to a promoter be on your game and exude energy, give compliments, recognize them and listen to them. You can be tactile with a promoter. Even a slap on the shoulder is seen as a type of recognition. Appropriate physical contact energizes them and makes them feel needed and recognized. Be witty, humorous and flexible. Don't be linear. Be lateral. Avoid talking down to them or patronizing them but handle the details for them. Show them how they can save effort. Make them look good and be careful with criticism. Give them the opportunity to be first in and head of the pack. Carefully keep them focused because they will distract you consciously or unconsciously.

A team of sellers with these personality styles pretty much covers all of the bases. The key then is to subtly adapt your team to the style of buyer. It's not about changing who you are, rather it is about appealing to the personality styles and values of the client. About a 15% adaptation is enough and the personality shift is more subtle than you might think. After all, the client is probably talking to you because you have something unique that they need. They are not expecting you to be just like them, but they need to be able to relate to you.

The key is to not to wear your profile on your sleeve. Dim the extremes of your style a bit. If you are a naturally loud person, keep your voice a little lower than usual, and don't start off your meeting with a joke. Tone down a bit. Be personable but not too intimate. And bear in mind that these subtle personality-style shifts are much easier to do when you are listening because neutral is easier. You must observe. You can sit back and analyze the profile of the person across the table from you and observe what questions they ask. From there, you can make your subtle shifts to appeal to their values and communication style.

Just so you know, I am a promoter. I usually talk big picture and like to create and have fun.

At one presentation I gave, a CEO got up right in the middle of my talk and walked out, but not before saying he was interested in what I was offering and would get in touch. I called and suggested lunch on me at one of the more expensive restaurants

His reply was "let's go to the little café on the corner because it is close to my office and good enough."

From that, I made the assumption that he was probably a controller. He was looking for a place efficiently close to his office. Frills and trends are not bottom-line enough for a controller.

I sat down with him over a quick lunch, wasn't too chatty and asked bottom-line questions. I pulled out some testimonials and offered to walk-and-talk him back to his office to save time. I showed him results with the testimonials. I got to the point and I respected his timelines; all key values of a controller.

In group presentations, therefore, you can see how important it is to integrate all personality styles into the presentation. Give bottom line info, then a fun story, then a heartfelt one, then crunch numbers. By doing this, we meet the needs of all the styles in the room.

X.
Your Inner Circle

Leonard Brody is a leading advisor to high-tech startups and Fortune 500s in the area of e-business entrepreneurism. I once heard him give a sobering speech to a group of would-be entrepreneurs about three questions that will be asked by venture capitalists before they even read a business plan:

1. Is it a pet rock or a pill? If someone presented a pet rock; something nice to have, cute but without a business role, then it wasn't financeable. However, if a business idea was a pill of sorts, in other words was a critical solution to a business pain or challenge, the deal was financeable.

2. Who is the market and who are the competitors? If the answer is 'everyone is a client and there are no competitors,' the VCs know the team has not done its due diligence and is living a pipe dream.

3. Has the CEO pulled together a team that is even brighter than themselves? CEOs who need to be the brightest in the room all the time will surround themselves with sycophants and yes-people, which kills innovation and leadership.

Not unlike successful CEOs who surround themselves with people who are smarter than them, successful big deal closers know how to assemble an inner circle of advisors. The people in their inner circle include mentors, lawyers, bankers, foreign exchange advisors, accountants and financial advisors.

In my opinion the most crucial member of your inner circle is your mentor. Mentors are important to check in with on a formal or informal basis. They are the people who can point out where short-term gains can become long-term losses. A mentor can evaluate the situation, see what worked in the past and give sage advice. A sober second thought can save money and careers.

One of my mentors, Jim Janz, has helped over 50 people in the past 30 years become millionaires; some of them are millionaires ten times over. I had the opportunity to assist Jim in launching his network distribution organization in South Africa in 1997/98. Several years before, Jim gave me one of my first paid speaking engagements in Bellingham, Washington, addressing a group of his team leaders.

Trevor and I interviewed Jim Janz for this book and asked him to talk about how one can find a great mentor and get the most out of the mentoring relationship:

Jim Janz on mentoring

"Some people have many mentors. Some people have one mentor. It depends on the scope of their life. If the scope is enormous, you need more than one mentor because you need a mentor that understands the business side of your life, the spiritual side, the family side and so on.

They may be there simultaneously or they may be there at various stages of your life, because the mentor you had when you were starting out may not be the mentor you need down the road a ways. Boiled down, mentoring is about going someplace you haven't been before with someone who has already been there.

You should be wary of getting stuck in a mentorship situation that is no longer of value to you. Be aware that you may grow past your mentor. You want a mentor who is where you want to be. That mentor should be someone you want to emulate; someone who has achieved the same things you want to achieve.

My mentor is someone I have spent a lot of time with and who mentored me specifically on always having a new dream. The first time I met (minister and author) Dr (Robert) Schuller, he was backstage in Chicago, sitting under a little light studying his notes before he went on stage to address this huge audience. My company had just achieved some rather spectacular success, and were enjoying some of the highest recognition to be achieved in our industry.

[Author's note: Within a few short years Jim had managed to build a sales organization comprising tens of thousands of distributors throughout North America. Three decades later, in 1994 when I met Jim, he and his wife Sharon had over 500,000 people in their organization and it spanned Holland to Japan and everywhere in between. That year his estimated group revenues were over $1 billion.]

I was there to speak with him because I had referred to him so many times in my previous speeches that it was decided that we would speak together. So I went up to him and said "you must be Dr Schuller." He looked up and said, "you must be Jim Janz. What's your new dream."

I laughed but hesitated and he told me that you should always have your new dream on the tip of your tongue. I will never forget that.

A lot of people think that when they reach a certain stage in life that they no longer need to have those forward-looking ideas anymore. Wrong. Dr Schuller is in his late 70s and he has as many dreams as he had when he was 19.

In this case he is a mentor and a role model. Sometimes role models become mentors that you never talk to. I have mentors that I read every day. Some of them are dead but they are still mentors: I read their books every day to keep me focused on the things I want to accomplish.

In the context of mentoring, here is what not to do: don't call somebody up and ask them to mentor you. I hate that when someone does that to me. I have had guys I knew well that I had to turn down.

There are two things to do in finding a mentor. Number one, find a way to do something for them.

Number two find a reason, a legitimate reason, to get together with them to talk about something that has nothing to do with them mentoring you.

You may discover that you didn't want them to mentor you at all: a lot of people look better in the distance as opposed to close up.

Most of the people who become mentors are involved in causes. They are into committees, programs, philanthropy deals, all that kind of stuff. Call them up. Tell them you want to get involved, that you are a team leader and want to help out even if you just carry the bags.

You find a connecting point. There isn't a whole lot you can do for a Jimmy Pattison (Canada's billionaire automotive and media mogul), but when someone like that is being interviewed on the radio or something, and they say they want to make something happen for one of their causes, the bell goes off in your head and you find a way to connect.

(The mentor relationship) follows the phrase, when the student is ready, the teacher will appear.

So, let's say you have established a relationship and want to build on it. You have to be ready to learn. You have to be ready to ask questions, listen very well and not argue.

You have to understand that you will have to put aside some of your opinions and preconceptions if you are going to be successfully mentored by this person. There are a lot of adjustments you may have to make.

I took a large organization and melded it into a larger one. I had been the sole leader of that organization for over 30 years and then became subservient to that organization's board of directors, of which I was a member. First off, I threw out over $80,000 of my own material even though some of it was better than what they had. **I did that because I needed what they had more than I needed what I had.** I had to put aside what I thought was right in order to be mentored.

For a long time I was the new guy on the block, even though I was more experienced than most of the guys on the board. I had to swallow it. I had to shut up and pay attention and listen.

Basically it is an attitude that involves a willingness to learn as well as a desire to change what you think is right in your life."

Lawyer

Having your own lawyer is crucial. One does not want to resort to thumbing though the yellow pages at the last minute. You should develop a good, close personal relationship with a lawyer as soon as possible. This will allow you to see him or her on very short notice. At some point you will have to be able to act quickly to close a big deal, and you will need your lawyer to drop what they are doing and move as quickly as you are moving.

Select a lawyer using three criteria: someone that you can work with; someone who has good knowledge of your business, and; someone who is capable of thinking outside the box. Big deals sometimes require creativity, and your lawyer should be able to come up with creative solutions rather than just following precedent. Bear in mind that your lawyer is in many ways a reflection of you and how you do business, so you want someone on your team who has a good personality and who can get along with people. If your lawyer is not a good fit with the people you are dealing with, he or she could kill the deal before you get started. Pick a lawyer who will be a deal-maker for you, not a deal-breaker.

What is communicated in the boardroom and the actual language of the contract can sometimes turn out to be quite different. A contract can drastically affect your profit margins, so a commercial lawyer can be a great asset. And a good tax lawyer can reduce your exposure to capital gains taxes, which can affect your bottom line and in some cases mean the difference between you making a profit or a loss.

If you select a lawyer from a large firm, you could be paying large dollars but be deemed small potatoes in the grand scheme of things at that firm, and therefore given small priority. Big-firm lawyers usually charge by the hour. Some have pressure from their partners to bill by the minute and meet a minimum quota of billable hours to cover their big overhead costs. If your deal does not go through, you may be stuck with a big legal bill regardless.

A lawyer in a smaller firm may not have the high overhead and may want your business more. They may be willing to be more flexible in their billings. In either case, you should always discuss the legal costs in advance or have a prior arrangement with your lawyer so that you know what to expect if the deal does not proceed. Bear in mind the advantages of having an experienced, below the radar lawyer in a small firm who can get things done quickly and often has great connections. A high-powered lawyer who is on everyone's radar screen could scare your client away or at least make them more defensive from a legal aspect.

I have an agreement with my lawyer to run any deal by him. Sometimes there is one line in a contract that can change its whole direction. If you are not a legal expert you can miss these small details. Many times I have been unable to solve a business problem and have talked to my lawyer, who always seems to find a creative solution I wouldn't have thought of on my own.

Simply put: good lawyers are good problem solvers and great assets for your team.

Banker

Establish two solid relationships with bankers or banking teams. It is important to have several sources for financing. Some deals are less traditional and more risky than others. If you have only one relationship with a traditional bank and haven't established relationships with venture capitalists, angel financiers and other sources of financing, your deal could be stopped dead in its tracks.

Through a solid commercial banker, you may be able to find some of the key players for your inner circle, including lawyers, mortgage brokers, etc. Your banker will often be keen to introduce you to their own team because it is likely to increase their chance of being asked to finance your next deal.

A rule of thumb for working with bankers is always to deal with the main branch. If you need decisions on the fly, you can walk upstairs to get to a manager. Remember the eight-minute rule: If you create enough of a clamour for at least eight minutes, you will get the manager.

For a backup banking and finance team, find another bank or credit union that you like, get an account with a credit card and make a couple of deposits. Have lunch with them. Tell them they are the backup to your main banking source. Nurture this relationship and you will gain bargaining power with your main bank because all of a sudden you have an alternative.

Michael Barker-Fyfe on Foreign Exchange

Bill Gibson closed a deal for KBI a few years ago for C$1.8 million to train sales reps for one of the top insurers in South Africa. They asked us to convert the amount into rands in the contract. Day after day, Bill and I painfully revised the contract in an attempt to meet the needs of their legal department. We didn't know that the rand was likely to lose value rapidly for the foreseeable future. There was eventually a two-month delay between closing the deal and the finalized contract. Our deal was watered down to $1.2 million, for a net loss of $600,000 before we even started.

If you are doing business in foreign countries, it is critical to align yourself with a reputable and technologically savvy foreign exchange company.

Michael Barker-Fyfe manages corporate business development for the Vancouver office of Custom House Global Foreign Exchange. Custom House has 80 offices around the world and completes over $10 billion in foreign exchange transactions each year.

We asked his perspective on the importance of forex advice:

Why would a big deal closer use a company like yours and not a bank?

Because we specialize in foreign exchange and offer services and products that banks do not. It's telling that banks often refer clients to us and we count many bankers as clients.

How have you seen good deals go bad when the forex isn't handled properly?

Many times we hear horror stories of deals that fall apart, parties getting sued and individuals or businesses losing money. A classic example is non-resident buyers of property in Canada. They typically depend on their foreign bank to exchange currencies and wire funds to the trust account in Canada. What often happens is the funds get delayed, and because of the legal duty to inform all parties, the seller may decide to walk away from the deal due to late payment. We've seen foreign banks take over a week to get funds to the trust account. This is due to their cumbersome and time-consuming process of wiring money. Our direct wire platform allows us to move the funds faster, and we'll save clients money while providing better service and market information.

Is there a way for people to get a quick thumbnail sketch of how forex works before they consult a forex professional? (sources, sites, books etc.)

Forex is a small piece of the puzzle and it's a difficult area to become an expert in quickly, so I would suggest a consultation with someone in our industry. Xe.com is a popular site for crossrates and you can visit customhouse.com for an overview of our services.

What have you done to cater to deal brokers to help their deals run more smoothly?

One example is land developers who use our services to pay for foreign products or convert foreign receivables. If they also market the properties they develop, they see the benefit of our service for non-resident buyers and put (these non-resident buyers) in touch with us. There are many examples of these types of deal brokers, such as lawyers, financial planners, boat brokers, fine art dealers, project marketers and realtors. They either use our services or direct their clients to us as a value-added. They recognize the importance of dealing with a specialist.

When in the process of a deal should the forex expert be consulted?

I would suggest speaking to someone early on so you know how best to approach it. Every situation is different and currency markets are volatile, so it's prudent to have a game plan early.

Have you seen many big deals (over $1,000,000) involving forex?

Clients can fix an exchange rate for a big deal in advance with a forward contract to protect against fluctuations in currency markets. Let's say a client wants to buy a container of product overseas. They can fix the price at the time of the order so that they know exactly what the cost of goods will be and they can protect their margins.

In early 2004, one of our clients contacted us to sell US$5 million over the next five months. There are a few ways of doing this, but the two most common ways are open contracts (which can be exercised at any time during the duration) and closed (which can only be exercised on the final day of the contract term).

Most people book open contracts for flexibility, but closed contracts offer a slightly better price. In this case, we consulted with the client and found that they could comfortably book five US$1 million closed contracts out in a ladder formation over the next five months. That is, the first contract would be due in a month, the second in two months and so on. Because closed forwards are priced better, we saved our client C$21,000 over the term of this arrangement, just by suggesting this approach.

What else should people know about forex?

Foreign exchange isn't just about exchange rates. Clients can be so focused on price that they miss the big picture. It's about information, service and innovative products. As to the big picture, it's important to know that you're dealing with a foreign exchange brokerage that complies with international regulations regarding the transfer of money. This protects the forex specialist and the client, and is an important issue that is often overlooked."

An added benefit to using someone like Custom House is the level of due diligence they perform on all parties involved in a transaction. Michael told of several instances where they were able to steer a client away from a potentially bad deal after looking into the third party. Due diligence can be done by any party involved in a deal, and can identify other parties involved that are acting in bad faith, thus saving money, time and credibility.

Accountant

You need a good accountant. There is a common mentality that the solution to life is simply to make more money and hang onto it. But few have actually saved their way to riches. But foolishly handing over more money than you have to is stupid. You wouldn't do it in a store, so why are you doing it as a citizen?

By all means pay the legal amount of tax that is the government's due, but be aware that a good accountant can maximize deductions. As a big deal closer, some years will be good and some will be a bit lean. A good accountant can find legal but creative ways to reduce taxes paid in the big years so you can ride out the lean years.

Look for an accountant who works with other companies in your business. They will have developed expertise in the industry and can act as excellent sounding boards. If you don't have a good accountant already, go to some of the key players in your inner circle and see if they can find you one. But be careful of working with an accountant who is a little too creative. If they are prone to cooking your books, they will be at the stove with the rest of their clients as well, so when the audit comes down, you are also in the net.

The lawyer and accountant may appear to be at cross-purposes or, at times, actually duplicating their efforts. So, a quick breakdown of duties:

An accountant will tell you how to structure your company for tax writeoffs. A tax lawyer will look it over and rejig the structure because they are experts at case law and precedent. The accountant is looking at the theory. The lawyer has been to court fighting for, and over, business entities and knows how business structuring can get dirty. Anytime you restructure to reduce your exposure to tax, you walk a fine line between good ethics and legalities, and fraud. Your accountant can give you advice and is an expert on business structuring. Your lawyer can determine the legality of the structure. Your lawyer has a liability insurance fund. Your accountant does not.

By the same token, your financial planner will throw ideas around on business structures as well, often focused on retirement and succession. In this case too, your lawyer can say what actually is legal and why.

If your accountant and lawyer are best friends, they might be less apt to argue a point on your behalf between each other or run up a red flag about each others' actions.

Financial planner

'Financial planner' is a broadly misused term. They are neither mutual fund hucksters, nor insurance sellers who take orders. A financial planner evaluates your financial situation and helps you invest in a broad range of financial and insurance products.

Your financial planner may be your only point of contact to a full network. Chances are good that your planner has a full toolkit of professionals backing him or her up, and will give you access to their accountant, tax lawyer, etc.

Don't neglect your due diligence though. It needs to become evident that your financial planners' top goal is your benefit. You have to be number one. Make sure they are not biased by financial or insurance instruments they are selling. Get comparisons to other instruments and alternatives.

XI.
The "Instant Success" Trap

We have all heard the stories about lottery winners who make the big score but are then filing for bankruptcy a couple of years later.

One of the reasons is that they have acquired instant financial success without understanding the principles of accumulating and maintaining wealth. Inside they often feel that they will have yet another windfall. High-risk investments, poorly chosen financial advisors and over-generosity with family and friends often leads them to financial ruin. Sound investment strategies, the ability to manage cash flow, healthy levels of caution and even mild paranoia are tools we all need to succeed financially. Yet, often after a big win, people are overoptimistic about how soon the next one is coming. The big win analogy applies just as well to big deals.

The sales manager at my first sales job once sat me down with a gloomy look on his face within three months of working there. His concern was my relatively instant success. My monthly sales quota was $25,000 in advertising sales, and within a two-week period I closed one deal for $210,000 within three calls and another deal for $50,000 within two calls on the client.

His concern was that I hadn't really even developed a strong routine or sales process, and both deals came from people I had previous relationships with. He warned me that the next couple of deals may not just land in my lap and that it takes a plan and the discipline to follow that plan to create long-term success. I looked at him as if he had three heads, and explained to him my background and ability to network into these deals using skill of persuasion and in-depth knowledge of the advertising industry – all 90 days of it!

My next month I landed a deal for $20,000 and the following month I battled to hit $10,000. He was right. My motivation plummeted, and so did my credibility. Once my ego was deflated back to mortal proportions, I emotionally limped back into his office and meekly asked about that sales process he mentioned.

It took me several months to begin busting quotas again. This time it was with a sound process and with less stress on me. I had learned the true process of not just hitting the big numbers but how to maintain them. When those big deals came in again, I didn't look at them as the mainstay of my commissioned income but a bonus, realizing that I have to actually eat between those big deals that come every three months.

Sometimes instant success results from one-off situations or unpredictable circumstances. My large advertising deals came about as a result of a sudden flurry of venture capital investments in a certain industry sector, so once the investing slowed so did the ad dollars. All of us have many opportunities like this in our career, and big deals are healthy, as long as we don't base our business model or long-term sales strategy on it. When the well dries up, do we have a strategy in hand to replace these revenues?

Ask yourself a couple of questions to ensure that you aren't falling into the big deal success trap:

- Are the majority of my sales coming as a result of a short-term circumstance that could shift or change in the near future?
- If I have been closing big deals lately, do I understand how I did it and can I duplicate this in the future?
- Am I just hoping that the business will keep rolling in like it has been, even though I am relatively undisciplined in my sales process?
- Is my business highly profitable yet has little to no competition in the marketplace?
- Do I consider myself luckier than talented or disciplined?

Answering "yes" to a couple of these questions means your long-term success may be in jeopardy.

Don't get me wrong. Short-term success is great, as long as we see it for what it is. If you know that the economy is extra hot, and what you have to offer is selling like crazy, there are two guidelines you can follow to translate short-term to long-term: Keep your expenses at pre-boom levels so you can bank your newfound windfall and be ahead of the game when the market returns to normal.

When you're hot and those deals are rolling in with little work, it's not time to coast. Take advantage of this finite boom time and sell harder and longer. I've seen people experience great success in business and right in the middle of the gold rush they go on a well-deserved holiday, only to return and find that the rush is over. You'll have lots of time to rest, plan and holiday when the flurry of selling slows. When you are on a roll, go faster and harder.

If your unexpected successes come from sources you didn't expect, keep selling in your traditional sectors and client groups in case this new niche has a short life. Take the time and effort to research your market in more depth. Also, see if you can use this as a learning experience to help you identify other niches or hidden opportunities in the future. Precedent can be a great teacher. Learn to read the signs so you can see around the next curve.

Be aware that there is a difference between a business model and a deal. A business model is a long-term profitable offering of a product or service to a specific market or markets, and long-term success is assured by having a unique and competitive offering. A deal, however, happens because an individual or a group of individuals make a deal with you because they need something you have. It may not be unique but opportunity has met preparedness and you fulfilled the order, with the result that you are able to put some cash in your pocket. This is not a business model. Resist the temptation to build a business around a deal.

XII.
And…The Close

Throughout this book we have discussed how closing big deals is a process, not an event. With that said, you will eventually find yourself leaving your client's office some day with a new relationship, a contract and a cheque. The big deal does indeed get closed.

That meeting is the time for you to deliver a believable, credible recommendation to your client. Your recommendation often will come in the form of a consultative close. Consulting only works when the consultant has a high level of credibility with and permission from the consulted to offer advice.

When you provide your recommendation, it should be obvious to your client that it is a culmination of your careful needs analysis and your understanding of their product, industry and solution.

Your recommendation ideally will summarize their core pains and goals. It will outline what they need using their language and value set.

You know your client's pains and goals better than they do because you have done a thorough needs analysis. You speak their language because you have identified their personality profiles. You know their values because you have put in the time to get the relationship to the commitment level and beyond.

In summarizing the key points of the deal that have already been agreed upon in previous discussions, you answer the client's question: What is in it for me? This is a true benefit statement that tells the client exactly what they are getting.

Take the fear out of yes

Sometimes the client knows logically that they are ready to buy. Emotionally, however, they are not prepared to take the leap. What we need to do here is remove the downside to yes. Sometimes saying no or just not making a decision appears to have all benefit and no risk, while yes seems to carry huge repercussions.

Find out what scares them about doing business with you. Then make that fear go away.

Your close will take the fear out of yes. Think about their possible objections in advance. Provide them with guarantees and assurances that lead them comfortably to conclude that yes is the safest bet. If you have to, develop a new product. Many technology products that corporations use today didn't evolve in a lab. They evolved from a core client fear. One specific fear commonly held by large companies and governments around the world led to the development of large-scale, multimillion dollar computer firewall technology and anti-virus systems. These companies knew that electronic intruders could bring their operations to a halt and their business to its knees. Governments knew that defending the secrets on their networks was literally a matter of life and death. Many of the big deal closers that met this demand are billionaires.

Think creatively, but don't feel that you have to solve world peace to get the big deal closed, however.

Ask your client for their business with conviction and a smile, and ask for it with the intention of being part of their business for a no less than a decade.

If the process has been followed, this final close should feel natural and happen naturally.

"As long as you're going to be thinking anyway, think big."

- Donald Trump

XIII.
Interviews with the Million Dollar Closers

The concepts we have discussed in this book are distilled from a decade of mentoring and being mentored by clients on three continents.

These concepts have come to light from formal meetings in the boardrooms of major corporations, as well as from rather more informal settings. One of our mentors shared his big deal insights from the back of an all-terrain vehicle on a game farm in South Africa.

Some of the best insights came after the wrap-up of a formal session with a client or prospect. Sensing that the executive still wanted to talk even though the meeting was done, I lingered in the office, ears open and mouth closed. Very rarely will you come across a person who is running a Fortune 500 company who isn't a wealth of information on closing big deals. Soak it in and take notes if you have to.

In the course of writing this book, and as we did the interviews that you are about to read, we found that the big deal closers we were speaking to had more in common than they had differences in their approaches to closing big deals.

These closers drove more depth and reality into the concepts we have discussed in the book.

Before interviewing Lisa Howell, we talked about adding value to every contact. With her team-selling approach and the personal value-added network she brings into every deal, she re-defined and emphasized for us what the term "value-added" means in closing big deals.

Before we met with Dak Molnar, we knew that confidence and credibility are keys to closing deals. But when we sat down with him, we were struck by how much his confidence filled the room and buoyed the conversation.

Before we had lunch with Willi Schmidt, we had been preaching the merits of focusing on present and long-term relationships with clients. Willi brought that point home, going so far as to print his home phone number on his business card. To paraphrase him, when his client wins, he wins.

Before interviewing Carey Healey we claimed that anyone can grow into becoming a big deal closer. Carey himself asked us why we were interviewing him. He happened to be an engineer who grew into a big deal closer. This non-sales type showed us how a client-focused and thorough engineer can become capable of garnering client trust and millions of dollars in business for his organization.

These are the stories of four big deal closers, in their own words.

LISA HOWELL
Senior Director of Strategic Business Sales, Medical Systems, Royal Philips Electronics

Philips, based in the Netherlands, is one of the world's biggest electronics companies, as well as the largest in Europe, with over 160,000 employees in over 60 countries. Philips Medical Systems is the single largest Philips business in the United States.

Tell us a bit about your industry and how you got into it.

I got into the industry not through any business drive but because I was a frustrated doctor. I wanted to get into medical school, but I started out of school selling for General Electric (GE) in the health-care environment, which is basically anything in a hospital that takes a picture, like CT scans, ultrasounds and scanners.

I started as an entry-level sales rep selling one CT, for example, to one hospital. Some people in my industry would argue that selling CTs is a complex sales process. I disagree because even though it is a million-dollar product, the transaction is in effect a glorified commodity sale because the basics of professional sales is the same.

So I was with GE nine years and have been with Philips now for five years. I went from regional sales specialist to regional sales manager and now to this (senior director) job.

There are really only three companies left in this industry: Philips, GE and Siemens. The consolidation of the industry down from seven players in the last five years has created the need for a more complex sell. This is because our customers aren't buying one machine any more, they are actually buying the relationship.

There really isn't much of a technical differentiation between the products. The act of faith really plays strongly in the health care world for a couple of reasons.

First, you are dealing with people's lives. Second, the people we are selling to are mostly clinicians and doctors, and they are not naturally good assessors of the technology. We are just enabling them to do their jobs, so they don't really, fundamentally know what they are buying. Finally, health care in the US and Canada is in crisis from a business point of view. People need this equipment, so there is great demand. So buying this stuff for $2 million is a whole lot more involved than figuring out what bandages your hospital is going to use. So people can really lose their job if they buy the wrong machine or if they go with the wrong company.

Now I run the sales force for North America in the Strategic Business Group. This group only came about two years ago, as buying decisions in hospitals were elevated from the department doctor level to the carpeted CEO level. They don't really care whose box they buy. They have to find vendors who will come in to work with them to meet some of their unmet needs that may or may not have to do with the technology that we sell.

So, we leverage the entire Philips portfolio, from medical to lighting to consumer electronics, to create enough value so that a hospital will sign multiple-year contracts to buy our boxes.

Can you give an example?

One of the biggest things that keeps hospital CEOs up at night is how to build more capacity, which means more bricks and mortar, more buildings, more beds. We have created a kind of voluntary consortium of industry leaders in all the fields involved in building a hospital, ranging from architecture to project managers to designers and builders. That way, we more or less own the management of those interactions. By doing this, we take twelve months off the building cycle for a 300-bed hospital. This is huge from a financial standpoint, as well as for capturing market share because the hospital CEO opens more beds sooner. Also, we make sure that the project stays within the budget, because we source all the equipment that goes into the hospital. Normally the equipment sourcing doesn't happen until month 18. But if we get all those people in the consortium to come together, we can solve a lot of problems from the start.

What kind of approach do you use to make sure you are assessing your client's core needs and tailoring a solution for them?

We have profiling tools that ask, for example, if the client currently has any of our equipment, if they like us, if we have a past relationship with them and if decisions are being made at executive level or at user level.

On a big deal there may be five or six Philips sales reps calling one hospital and a couple of our sales managers involved as well, so we all have to come together to document everything that the team knows about that client.

From there, we generally have enough information to go to the next step, which is an analysis of the unmet needs of the client. We listen to the executives or the decision-makers and wait for those unmet needs to bubble up. This means we have to listen carefully, which is sometimes hard for salespeople. That can lead to one of the biggest mistakes I have seen on big deals, which is trying to be all things to all people, solving all their woes.

One of the keys to our success is our ability to focus on two or three very discreet unmet needs and handle those very well, and then build a platform to uncover more unmet needs the next time around. Once we have that unmet needs meeting, we are at a decision point and we look in our bag of tricks full of value-added stuff for solutions that fit.

So once we have gone through the process of profiling the client, brought the team together for sort of an in-house kumbaya session to determine what we know about the client, had our unmet needs meeting with the decision makers and aligned the clients' unmet needs with our portfolio…to use a golf analogy, it's a pretty short putt (to the close).

The proposal process becomes really easy. In effect it's a confirmation proposal, not a sales proposal. The close should be anticlimactic. When we get the contract signed it's kind of exciting but it probably really happened about six months previously.

Let's talk about losing big deals. What are some of the things you see that can quickly sideline or finish off a big deal before it comes to fruition?

The painfully obvious one is when we try to close a big, complex deal two weeks before they are ready to make a decision. We call that spaghetti thrown on a wall (hoping something will stick). My group doesn't have any spaghetti. I don't really consider that a lost big deal, actually, because we shouldn't have been there in the first place.

That could actually be a situation where you are just brought in as a third bidder to round out the numbers...

Exactly. Another one happened this year, when we hung our hat on one particular hospital administrator. We were singing his song, he was singing ours. And then he got fired. When people change, it is really hard to maintain momentum if you don't have a broader influence base than the one point of contact.

Another thing is the ability to listen without filtering. The hardest thing for some salespeople is to shut up and listen to all the needs of a client instead of just the needs that they have the solutions to. For example, we don't have an IT system for sale and a competitor took a big deal away from us this year because we thought a $35 million diagnostic imaging system was this clients' big deal, while they were actually thinking of a $140 million IT system purchase. It is so hard to do, personally and in business, just to listen without filtering.

What about follow-up and follow-through without harassing the contact? How important is that? What tools do you use to maintain that contact?

Not to oversimplify it, but it goes back to the unfiltered listening concept. I don't get to that third or fourth meeting, or to the sweet spot eighth or ninth meeting unless I continue to have things to say that are interesting to them. So I don't talk about how many bits and bytes the scanner has. I talk about things like new Medicaid legislation that could have an impact on the industry.

So you have to relate to your client in terms of their knowledge base, not your own knowledge base that consists of, frankly, whatever you are selling. Also, each meeting should solve a problem and set up another meeting.

I am an advocate of doing two things well at a time. So if I can get one thing accomplished and get a commitment for a follow-up to do the second thing, I am happy. You could call it the sniper approach as opposed to the shotgun approach. The patience involved in creating the chain of events that brings you to the magical number of meetings involves discipline.

What are some of the characteristics of big deal closers?

Exquisite listening skills. Discipline in sticking to the plan and pacing the deal, in terms of follow-up and follow-through, to the close. The ability to do what you say you will do, and not commit to something you can't do. It comes back to my concept of doing two things really well. Another characteristic is the capacity to earn and sustain trust.

What do you think are the benchmarks needed to be reached to go from product peddler to trusted advisor?

I would say proven integrity. Such as referring a client to someone else if you don't have the product they need.

How important is your own personal team for closing big?

It's invaluable to have people like that. My father sells big capital equipment for Nortel. We talk to each other about our deals all the time. He is in sales but he has nothing to do with the medical industry, so he is objective enough to point out glaringly obvious next steps that I can't see because I am in too deep.

Our last question is meant to elicit an all-encompassing statement. Finish the sentence: to close bigger you need to…"

"…have closed the deal long before the champagne cork is popped."

DAK MOLNAR
Investment Division, Vancouver office, Colliers International

Colliers International is a global real estate services firm with 8,800 employees in 247 offices in 50 countries.

How and why did you get into the real estate industry?

My family. I grew up in a real estate family. The merits of the business were made clear at a young age. Ultimately I got into real estate seriously when I realized I was good at selling and talking. My mouth has always been my biggest asset.

I had an opportunity to sell some condominiums at age 19 or 20 and fell in love with it. I saw that people are comfortable with me and realized that people are my strongest asset.

Relationships are the strongest part of my life. Now I am not even 30 and I have an extremely wide-ranging network. It is actually humbling when you realize that you can pick up a phone and call such a wide range of people in the province, across Canada and around the world.

The reason I am in this business is because I like the relationships. You have to be into people to be in a people business.

What approach do you use to assess a client's core needs? How do you identify what they are really looking for? Basically how do you go from property peddler to trusted advisor?

In the beginning, people do business with you because you have a deal. I think a lot of people in this business don't view the transactional side and the repeat business side as important and I think that is a mistake.

They feel that the pool of business is so large that they can burn bridges with clients or not bother developing a good connection with a client for future business.

I find in my business that when I start with a client, I intend that this will be the first of many transactions. I spend a lot of time getting to know them and I spend a lot of time building the relationship around their needs.

I ask what were the deal motivators prior to us starting the relationship.

I put real, serious stock in understanding who I am working with. I profile them. I watch all of the small tiny little interactions that happen around them that other people would simply overlook because they think it isn't important.

It's not the dollars and cents in a deal. You have to remember that there are people in that building. You never know when you sell a building that there may be someone with a basic human conflict in there that has nothing to do with real estate that could kill your deal. It all starts with understanding relationships and values. Everything that people do in their lives, business and otherwise, is based on values. They bring that to work with them, they bring it home, to the park, the ski hill, you name it. It's not about widgets. It's about relationships.

What kills big deals?

I used to – and I think that this is what all young people in sales do – over-promise and under-deliver. If you tell a client something that you think may happen and you think may be true, but then doesn't, it squanders your credibility. A classic is the people that come in and hype a client up to the point where if one small thing goes wrong, the deal drops. They thought it was all blue sky.

The best way to do the right thing, which is under-promise and over-deliver, is to let a deal sell itself. Don't harp on about the crystal ball and go out on a limb and call it the greatest deal ever. All of those stereotypical things that salesmen say – that's what I try to avoid the most. Everybody starts hard-selling in this business. But they learn that more often the hard sell is a hard fall.

You have to arm your clients with the good and bad information and let them make the decision. It's their cheque and their risk.

All deals have some hair on them. I like to give bad news on Mondays and good news on Fridays.

You have to believe in yourself to close big deals. I always knew I was capable of doing big deals. There are people in this office who have been working here for 20 years and think the numbers in the deals I am doing are totally amazing. The sheer size of the numbers is intimidating for them. The only difference is the amount of zeroes. The risk is of course higher or lower, but the process is the same. It's a headspace. The (people who aren't closing big deals) don't look outside the box. People are as concerned about getting the goods they've been sold at a small level as at a big level.

Follow-up and follow-through. How do you do it without harassing your clients?

I call it the information game. I have clients who I contact daily, weekly, monthly. It's about passing useful information. If you are speaking to someone on a regular basis you should expand the focus of your relationship without losing focus on the common goal – which is business. You are just giving them information, without harassing.

It is basically keeping some realness to it, and not sounding like a broken record trying to close deals all the time asking the sales questions. You have to ask those questions but you should ask them in the context of life. I find that the less I push the more business I get.

What are the characteristics of big deal closers?

One of my mentors does something like $1 billion a year in business and he is so personable. (Big deal closers) have to be extroverted, but they have to be the kind of people that when they speak, people listen. The ultimate thing is that they have a personality that shines a little bit brighter than others. That comes from confidence. Not in an arrogant or egotistical way. There are no parameters on their personalities.

With the big deal guys, they have the confidence to share any and all info, within reason of course, with anyone else because they know that they will keep on closing big deals. Big deal closers are better communicators.

How important is your own team in closing big deals?

Everyone needs to be confident. If one of us is not confident, that lack of confidence will spread like cancer. I don't get stressed. The night before a big deal, I sleep. I prefer to work in an efficient, stress-free environment.

You need to depend on people, and of course your people have to be dependable. I don't like weakness. It drives me crazy. I think that is one of the big things on a big deal. If your client thinks that you are weak or scared, it's over. You're finished. You believe it, your team believes in it, so the whole thing, start to finish, flows

As for an external team, I have created my own team. I have two lawyers, I have two accountants I look to for tax issues and capital gains, I have an analyst on the stock market. I can translate to my clients what my stock market buddy is telling me about the capital markets, currencies, the Dow, gold, the way the wind blows in that industry.

My external team is up to 50 people who span different industries and both municipal and provincial politics. I belong to the urban development institute, the board of trade, the Young Entrepreneurs Organization. I network and share information through these people.

Most people don't have that sort of network to call on and rely on. They are not building relationships. I have spent more time building relationships than I have building my business. There have been one or two years when that has hurt me on a fiscal basis. But my relationships are stronger than a lot of business leaders who have been here for 20 years and who could buy and sell me 20 times over. But I can make things happen and pull the strings that need to be pulled. That is the best thing you can do in your twenties. Build your relationships for life.

Once they exist, the business you can drive out of that is incredible. What do you do when you build this business but you don't know anybody? If you are on an island by yourself you can't talk to anybody. You make mistakes and you talk to the wrong guys. At the end of the day, the deals will come by building relationships and networks.

If you weren't in this business what would you be doing?

I would be an entrepreneur. I would be selling some kind of widget or creating value in some kind of business. I would be manufacturing, creating or selling something. A product or service. With relationships attached of course.

To be a big deal closer, you have to…

"…be confident."

WILLI SCHMIDT
Major Accounts Manager, Finning Canada

Edmonton, Alberta-based Finning (Canada) sells, services and finances the full line of Caterpillar and complementary equipment throughout British Columbia, Alberta, Yukon, and the Northwest Territories. Finning (Canada) is a division of Finning International Inc., with principal markets in Western Canada, the United Kingdom and South America.

What are the keys to closing big deals?

You have to become a solution provider for the specific industry needs of that client. You have to build a relationship with all the players and then give them the solution to their challenges. Once you build a relationship, the order simply comes as an extension of that relationship. That is the biggest task in closing. Price really has nothing to do with it. The cost of the equipment is similar (to that of competitors). Our effort goes toward making the client understand the value that we add. Lots of people make large equipment. We are successful because we add value.

How did you get into the industry?

I started out as a trainer of mechanics. I am a licensed mechanic myself. I have an engineering background, and from that I found that I was logical and technology-oriented. In large equipment, having technical knowledge of what the equipment can do is big advantage.

There is an old adage, which I don't particularly agree with, that says that a salesperson only needs to know enough to sell the product. I am definitely not hearing that from you.

Absolutely not enough. You have to understand the equipment and you have to understand what it can do. The sale of the equipment is only the first step. Anyone can discount and get the first deal. The second deal depends on how well you manage the customer after the first deal. We pride ourselves on our ability to achieve regular repeat business.

I have only really been in the big deal business for the last four years. I started doing $4 and $5 million dollars a year. Looking at 2005, the projection is $50 million to $60 million dollars a year with the same customer base. We gained success in a number of ways. The customer has improved his position in the marketplace and that has created more work, which requires more equipment. I'd like to think we have helped him reach that stage by making him more efficient.

What is your approach to assessing the needs of your client?

My approach to assessing core needs is making sure we get all the input from all of the players. That is all levels in the company, from the president on down to the managers. My job is to determine their needs and learn their vision for their short- and long-term goals. If I don't understand their vision, it is very difficult for me to come up with a plan that will have the equipment I think they will need ready for them. We have regular meetings with all those people, we interact socially, then we make plans based on what we think their needs are in drawing up our forecasts.

What are the things you see that are losing big deals.

You're not close enough to the customer. There are always the challenges of pricing and supply. If we lose a deal where we have the availability and have met the timeliness standards, we do an autopsy and analyse why we lost the deal. We interview the customer and find out why we lost them. We isolate the issue and resolve it. If price-related, so be it; that's the way life is. If it's service, we can do something about that. Maybe we need additional training, more facilities.... We address that.

How has your behaviour and style changed since the days before you were closing big deals?

My role when we were selling a few million dollars a year was simply meeting with an equipment manager and servicing the short-term needs of his company. Since we have gotten bigger, my relationship with the president of the company has matured. Now we meet every few weeks. I have regular meetings with the GMs and VPs to understand what their bidding plans are. This allows me to better make my forecasts. We are doing better as a result. The relationship grows with the entire company rather than one or two people.

What are some of the characteristics of big deal closers.

A confident presenter of information. A high level of technical knowledge. A personality that is easy for someone to talk to and that takes rejection well.

You have to have all the information. I don't know anything about finance, but we have lots of people that do. I bring that guy in, I bring in the service guy. I am the facilitator for that client. I am the one he calls and I am the one who fixes things for him. Once you establish that you are ethical and fair, and you prove that you are going to resolve issues in a timely manner, you are going to close big deals.

Also, you have to realize that you will have to stand up and say "no" sometimes. That is part of being in on big deals. The customer must be brought to the realization that you are both ethical and fair.

You have to take the time and work to understand what they actually do and how they make their money. You need to solve the problem for the customer.

You absolutely have to have a trusting, ethical relationship. You have to answer your customer's questions as quickly as possible with as much passion as possible. That gets you on his A-list. From there you have to continually prove yourself capable of delivering.

You have mentioned passion twice in this interview. Describe your concept of passion as it defines a big deal closer.

There are some salespeople that are done at five every day and turn off their cellphones and that's it. My customer can get a hold of me anytime. One of the reasons is because I love this business. I have been doing this for 35 years and I understand it very well. There is a real joy to me in providing that level of service to the customer. I have this feeling that when he is happy, it makes me happy. That is what I mean by passion. That is what I feel. You are willing to go that extra mile not for the commission and not for the money, but to see the customer successful.

You can see yourself on the same path as your customer. There is no leap of faith to make because the faith is already there.

My goal and his goal are exactly the same. To make him successful. And if he is successful, I am successful.

(Willi has five contact numbers on his card. The last one is his home number.)

To be a big deal closer, you have to...

"...provide solutions."

CAREY HEALEY
Vice President, Sales, Infosat Communications

Infosat is a satellite telecommunications company based in Coquitlam, British Columbia. Their product line includes fixed and portable satellite communications products for construction, emergency, forestry, marine, mining, oil and gas, trucking, utilities, healthcare, remote communities and government. Infosat is a subsidiary of Bell Canada Enterprises, Canada's largest communications company.

Tell us about your approach to closing big deals.

For many of my clients, there are high-value reasons to be in remote places. These are multi-year, multiple-location deals. We have glossy brochures and whatnot but they ain't the real deal. At the end of the day, it's 'can you do it.' I can write the most detailed contract in the world and there will still be gaps in there where it comes down to trust. I am saying that I will do what I have said I will do.

In all my years here we have never been litigated against nor have we initiated litigation against anyone. We take the high road and our clients take the high road. When you come to something that could lead to a dispute, you pick the phone and say, "How do we get beyond this?"

How important is it to maintain a network?

I will answer that by starting with a story. There is this little company in Calgary I have always wanted to do business with ever since I met the guy in 1997 through a pilot project. He makes terminals that could connect through our boxes. I stop in and see him once a year and invite him to our company Christmas party. Turns out this year that there is a huge customer in the US that he is doing business with that is interested in doing business with us.

The point here is, the train only comes around the station once in a while in this business. You better make sure you are there.

Another thing is, in our business, if you need satellite, you just need it. If you don't, you don't. I don't know how many times I tell people they just need cellular or whatever. I have become like an anti-sales guy. But by doing that I think I build trust with people, by being honest that way. That is where the contrary approach works.

Eventually water finds its level. If you sell something to a client that they don't need, it is going to be showing up on your loading dock again in a couple of months. You want to make sure you are working on the right deals.

What have you learned from deals that don't pan out?

You have to lose some to know what it takes to win one. You would love to be cranky about (losing a deal), but if you stay in touch, be cordial and see what (the client will) want next year, you will get a deal down the road.

You also want to have no regrets when you are done, even if you lose the business. The way we do business here means there is usually nothing more we could have done to close that deal. We are competitive on our pricing, we have a good story to tell, great solutions…to use a sports analogy, we leave it all on the field. Sometimes there are other forces which dictate that the business moves in a different direction.

You mentioned earlier that curiosity can be a useful trait in closing big deals. Can you elaborate?

Curiosity helps a lot too. If you are curious as to why the client wants your product and how they will use it to take care of their clients, you can get insights that wouldn't ordinarily come through.

It is funny though. You would be surprised at how many people don't have that inquisitive streak. They are mechanical. That is my challenge when I am hiring salespeople. I ask them what rules they follow to sell. Then I ask them if they ever break the rules. I want to hear "yes." If the situation is right, if it will close the deal and if it will help the company, I want to hear "yes."

To be a big deal closer, you have to…

"…be curious, feel empowered to break the rules sometimes and be thorough."

Appendix

Big Deal Closer Self-Assessment

We have compiled a comprehensive 68-question self-assessment tool on closing large and complex deals.

It addresses 16 areas of competency and attitude. Even the most experienced and battle-hardened closers will fail to score high in all 16 areas. They will already know their strengths and use them to advantage. What sets them apart is that they have taken the next step in many cases and rounded off their weaknesses with tools, processes and people that mitigate the risks associated with those weaknesses.

This survey will allow you take a good look at your strengths and develop a plan to use your talents more effectively in closing big deals. Equally important is the capability to take a look at the areas where you are falling short. This will allow you to find the team, the process, the coach or the mentor that will take you to the next level.

Being a big deal closer isn't about having it all together or getting it together first thing next Monday morning. It is a process of development.

As with any goal, in order to get where you want to go, you first need to know where you are starting from in order to chart your path.

Big Deal Closer Self-Assessment

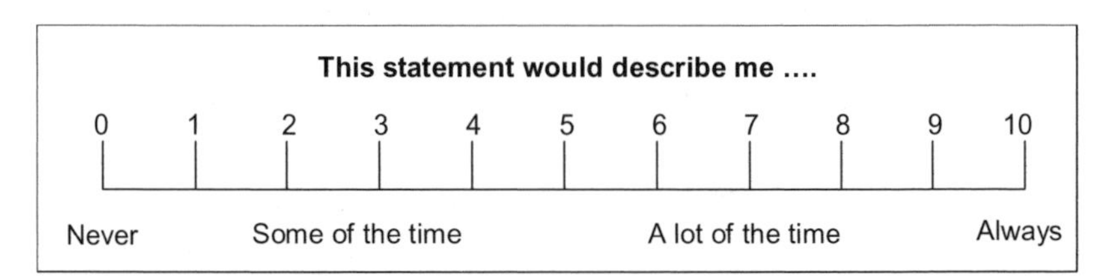

Question or Statement	Score (out of 10)
A master of basic selling skills	
1. I qualify prospects upfront, assessing their ability to purchase and invest.	
2. I assess the probability of the prospect choosing us as a vendor and adjust my investment in them accordingly.	
3. I am able to identify when there are opportunities to cross-sell, add-on, and up-sell.	
4. I know the common objections and concerns about my product and service offerings and either preemptively handle them or am prepared to effectively do so.	
5. I can recognize buying signals, both verbal and non-verbal.	
A problem solver	
6. I present my products and services as solutions to what I have identified as the pains and challenges of my clients.	
7. I am open-minded and put aside my bias and agenda in order to truly understand and comprehend client pains and challenges.	
8. I pull in internal and external resources to logically and laterally solve client challenges and problems.	
9. I apply my problem-solving skills to creatively find ways to be more effective as a salesperson and team member.	

A project coordinator	
10. I have a system of checks and balances to ensure that projects remain on track and on time.	
11. When supporting clients I systematically keep track of personal and corporate commitments to them and follow up with my team to ensure that we deliver what we promise.	
12. I effectively use a time management system and contact management programs to enable me to handle projects efficiently.	
An information gatherer	
13. I formally research client industries and companies before the call and periodically during the relationship.	
14. I use a good balance of mediums to research client industries and companies including the internet, news releases, industry periodicals, market reports and filings.	
15. I use non-formal mediums for research such as networking and information-sharing with vendors, salespeople, and individuals who are involved in my target industries and companies.	
16. I use a structured needs analysis process that explores all aspects of the clients' business and all applications of our solutions to their business.	
17. I am informally gathering client information and assessing needs in conversations and other communications.	
18. I am constantly educating myself on all of the products and services I sell, ensuring an ever increasing in-depth understanding of my offerings and their applications.	
A rapport builder	
19. I can identify a person's dominant personality style and shift my communications to appeal to their values and communications style.	
20. I am aware of peoples' posture, tonality, and level of extroversion, and adjust my communications style to make them comfortable.	
21. I am totally present and sincerely focused on people when we are communicating.	

A Competent Negotiator	
22. I rarely focus on price; I sell value, uniqueness, peace of mind, and the long-term relationship.	
23. I have a game plan before I start negotiating and know where the line is between a profitable, achievable deal and one that isn't worth doing.	
24. I don't take negatives, insults, or pressure personally and realize that these things may be a ploy to get me to drop my price or to lose my objectivity.	
25. I uncover the core needs, fears, goals, and interests in the deal early in the negotiations process. In turn this allows me to fashion and promote an agreement that the prospect will buy into.	
A customer-focused person	
26. I understand that being customer focused is not about pushing my agenda, it's about identifying what the client wants, their concept of credibility and timelines, and providing a solution that meets these factors.	
27. I have great after-sales service and monitor the client for future needs and challenges to ensure they are satisfied.	
28. I listen intently and search for the truth in client complaints and am humble and quick to remedy problems that may arise.	
A partner / team player	
29. I respect my support staff and senior executives. I only bring them in on a deal that is qualified; as well, I only bring them into meetings that are relevant.	
30. I am constantly communicating with and supporting my internal team.	
31. I recognize the other people that made the deal possible. Even though I earned the commission for closing the deal, I let my team know they are valuable.	
32. My clients don't see me as a salesperson but as a resource and a partner because of the strong team with which I am associated.	
A trainer / consultant / facilitator	
33. I can effectively teach/train clients to transfer the key knowledge for them to make an educated decision.	

34. I can engage a group of my peers and clients and facilitate a productive results-focused meeting.	
35. I can articulate my recommendations to clients in a clear and understandable way.	
A networker	
36. I am well connected to and trusted by the key players within my company.	
37. I am well connected to and trusted by the key players at my client companies.	
38. I am well connected to and trusted by the key players in my industry and community.	
39. I know that information is power and I am constantly searching for new and competitive ways to tap into profitable networks.	
40. I understand that for a good networker, being referable is much more important than gathering leads or referrals.	
An effective analyst	
41. Analysts take information gathering and networking to the next level, and as an analyst I understand what the information means and what key indicators to look for.	
42. In large complex sales or implementations, my technical knowledge and discernment are what make me a great partner and closer.	
43. I am an analyst, which takes me well beyond being a salesperson; in the eyes of the client I am seen as a trusted advisor.	
A good decision maker	
44. I know that people rarely have all of the information and analytics before making critical decisions, but I know when I have enough insight to make the right decision quickly.	
45. I am a rapid, accurate and confident decision maker.	
46. I tend to evaluate each choice in terms of its consequences. I use my standards and criteria to determine the pros and cons of each alternative.	
47. I translate my decisions into action quickly with a strong, well thought out implementation plan.	

48. I am able to articulate and garner support for my decisions from clients and from my team.	
A master presenter	
49. I am great at pitching groups of people on concepts in an engaging, upbeat, credible way.	
50. I read my audience and adjust my presentation style accordingly.	
51. I start strong, rapidly build rapport and leave the audience motivated to take the next step in the deal.	
52. I use visual aids and technology effectively in my presentations.	
53. Although I use visual aids, technology and handouts I make sure that I am the focus of the presentation; after all they are buying from me, not a Power Point.	
A master of proposals	
54. I deliver a customized relevant outline that is to the point and addresses key benefits, return on investment, and also builds confidence in me, my company, and my solution.	
55. I know that not every prospect or inquiry is qualified enough for me to invest the time to write an in-depth proposal, and I act accordingly.	
56. I have many uses for proposals including: to confirm a verbal agreement, a support document for a legal agreement, a road map for project management, or a stand-alone sales tool.	
57. My proposals enhance and accelerate the sales process toward a close.	
A credit manager	
58. I know the client business and their upside potential for revenues.	
59. I get to know which clients may pose a risk to the company if they are extending too much credit.	
60. At times I get involved in the collection process with my financial team, ensuring that they reach their desired goal and if at all possible keep the client as well.	

A listener	
61. About 70 % of my sales process is spent listening.	
62. I have tools for systematic listening such as needs analysis, client questionnaires, and customer service audits.	
63. I use questions that direct and guide the client to relay and communicate key information that will help build the relationship and prescribe the right solution.	
64. I give the client a chance to talk, think, and explore and they will often tell me what they want and need.	
A master of follow-up and follow-through	
65. I use frequent, value-added contact over a period of time that builds strong relationships with my clients.	
66. I have rapid follow-up after each key step in the sales process, often using a variety of mediums including e-mail, fax, mail, telephone, visits and calls from my team.	
67. I have a system in place that ensures that I contact key accounts on a regular basis. This system, and not my emotional state, drives my sales process.	
68. I often pick up the phone or send an e-mail or letter to a client just to let them know I've been thinking about them. I don't confine my calls solely to sales activity.	

Notes, Comments and Personal Action Steps:

____

____

____

____

____

____

____

ABOUT THE AUTHORS

Shane Gibson

Shane Gibson is an internationally recognized speaker, trainer and entrepreneur who has addressed several thousand people over the past decade in Canada, the US and South Africa. He combines a diverse background in sales force leadership, new entrepreneur development and extensive sales and leadership coaching. Shane is a contributing author to Knowledge Brokers International (KBI) Ltd.'s **The Complete Sales Action System™** and a master trainer in the **Managing Complex Business Relationships System**. Shane is executive vice president of KBI and heads the firm's North American operations.

He has been published in numerous publications on the topics of Leadership, Marketing, Sales, Strategic Communications and Assessing Business Opportunities. He has also addressed the topic of Entrepreneurial Leadership in magazine, radio and television interviews, including Financial Post and Profit Magazine.

He continues to advise a select group of business executives, sales professionals and entrepreneurs on personal sales performance and business. He is also in the trenches himself every day, selling and marketing KBI's solutions.

Internationally, KBI has implemented large-scale sales performance programs with SAB Miller, SIEMENS Industry and Transport Division, ACER Computers, BMW, Vodacom, and dozens of major financial services companies on three continents.

Shane's North American clients include: the Vancouver Board of Trade; Sauder School of Business; The University of British Columbia; Pacific International Securities; The University of Victoria; Fitness World; InfoSat Communications; ALS Environmental; The BC Automotive Retailers Association; YWCA; Dye & Durham; The Brick; Cendant Rent A Car (AVIS Rent A Car and Budget Rent-a-Car); Budget Rent-a-Car of Canada; The Financial Advisors Network; The Pacific National Exhibition; Travel Insurance Coordinators & Trent Health; TOS Insurance/Hub International.

Trevor Greene

Trevor Greene is a dynamic, innovative and well-traveled individual with over 15 years of experience in writing and reporting. He is a speaker of three languages, a published author, an entrepreneur, a trained and experienced liaison officer, and has eight years of highly regarded service in the Canadian Armed Forces.

Greene is a graduate of the University of King's College in Halifax with a Bachelor of Journalism (Honours). After graduation he spent seven years in Japan, working as a business journalist with the Tokyo bureau of Bloomberg News and Japan's largest newspaper, the Yomiuri Shimbun. He went on to write a book about Japan's homeless and then worked as a research editor with the securities branch of a UK investment bank.

Greene returned to Canada in 1995 to join the Royal Canadian Navy, going on to cross the Pacific Ocean to Australia in the Navy's sail training tall ship HMCS Oriole. After settling in Vancouver and transferring to the army reserves, Greene joined the Vancouver bureau of Bloomberg News as a general assignment reporter on business and finance in Canada and Asia. He also began researching and writing about the so-called poorest postal code in Canada; Vancouver's Downtown Eastside. He wrote his first nonfiction book in Canada, Bad Date: The Lost Girls of Vancouver's Low Track, about the women who have gone missing from the Downtown Eastside over the past 15 years. Bad Date was published in November 2001. Some of his present entrepreneurial projects include an eco-tourism venture and a community volunteer consulting company.

Greene is an officer in the Seaforth Highlanders, a Vancouver-based primary reserve infantry unit, where his main duties are domestic emergency and disaster response, and community and civilian agency liaison. At time of writing he was also preparing for a six-month army deployment to Afghanistan in 2006 as part of Operation Archer.

Greene lives on a boat docked at Fisherman's Wharf on Vancouver's Granville Island. He speaks Japanese and French.

Closing Bigger Resources

Take your sales performance to the next level

After working in the sales performance industry with literally thousands of professionals, managers and leaders, we can guarantee that this book will elevate your knowledge, wisdom and capacity to immediately boost your sales performance in record time. There is one other guarantee we can also provide, and that is that this is just the beginning of your journey to big deal closer status. There is no replacement for continuous, lifelong learning no matter what level of experience, knowledge or success you have attained.

When we do a sales performance improvement program for a client company it isn't about the material delivered to the sales team; it's about their ability to implement it tomorrow. Trevor and I have developed a number of resources intended to help you continue your path of development toward closing bigger. Following are some of the resources and programs available to you from Knowledge Brokers International and Closingbigger.com:

Closing Bigger Sales and Executive Coaching Programs

We wrote this book to fill a need in the marketplace. We found that many of our clients were in search of a resource on how to close big deals. Simply put, there were no "schools for big deal closers" and no organized mentoring and coaching processes either. Our experience and research for Closing Bigger led us to discover that most big deal closers developed their skills and insight through trial and error or ad hoc mentorship.

We have found that clients who have invested in coaching to help reinforce training and development programs have enjoyed a much higher success rate in implementing effective change. In order to provide more structured and dynamic mentorship and help implement change, we have put together the Closing Bigger Coaching Program.

Our certified Closing Bigger Coaches come from a wide variety of industries and disciplines. We have selected them to help coach you through the big deals and the process of becoming a big deal closer, be it in the heat of battle as the close gets near or even before the first business card has been exchanged. They have thousands of hours of coaching under their belts and in addition to our program already have successful sales and business coaching practices. Your Closing Bigger coach will help you achieve the following:

- Quickly implement and apply the lessons of Closing Bigger;
- Begin closing bigger deals sooner;
- Identify core sales strengths and weaknesses, and build a plan to grow your strengths and reduce or neutralize what's holding you back from achieving success;
- Perform postmortems on deals gone bad to help you learn and improve your closing ratio;
- Maintain access to someone who is accountable to you, who is objective and who will tell you what you need to hear (for *your* best interest), and;
- Help you prepare for specific bids and sales opportunities

Packages start at $1500.00 per month. Visit the Closing Bigger website at http://www.closingbigger.com for more information, or call 604-331-4471.

Closing Bigger – Big Deal Closers e-zine and interviews

Every month we sit down with two multi-million dollar closers who in their own words distill their strategies for closing big deals. Each month we focus on a different industry and region to give you a global perspective on what it takes to succeed. By subscribing to this monthly Big Deal Closers e-zine you will have a constant stream of mentorship from some of the worlds best big deal closers.

$12.00 per month

Visit http://www.closingbigger.com to subscribe today

Training the trainer and customized sales performance programs for your organization

If you're looking for an in-depth sales performance program on Closing Bigger that you can run internally, this is the option for you. This program provides texts, trainers guides, learners guides and exercises, and a trainers boot camp delivered at the location of your choice. With years of experience across three continents, we can effectively customize this program to meet your unique corporate, regional and industry needs.

In addition to Closing Bigger we have developed and published over 30 modules on sales, leadership and communications.

Companies that have invested in Knowledge Brokers International customized training systems include: BMW SA, Siemens, ABSA Bank, Vodacom, ACER, BOE Bank, ABSA Bank, and dozens of other organizations.

Visit http://www.closingbigger.com for more information or call 604-331-4471

Here's what people say about our programs and their results:

Acer:

"...an 85% increase in sales year on year"

Bankfin:

"...an increase in leads and conversion into business"

ABSA – Vehicle & Asset Finance:

"In July (our sales team) performed above target by 181% and in August by an incredible 204%"

United Stations – P4 Radio Natal:

"...our forward sales for the first quarter 2004 are up by approximately 150% from the same period 2003"

Keynote Speeches and Seminars

Book Shane Gibson for your next conference. Shane has spoken to thousands of sales people, executives and entrepreneurs on stages in Canada, USA and southern Africa over the past 11 years. His presentation style is often described as engaging, down to earth and humorous, and the content he delivers is packed with real value and take-home tools and processes that impact your bottom line.

Topics Shane speaks on include:

- Closing bigger
- Targeting the right clients
- Executive presentation skills
- Sales rapport
- Selling with your sales style
- Sales for non-sales types
- Executive leadership and coaching skills
- Entrepreneurial Jujitsu (peak performance and goal setting)

Visit
http://www.closingbigger.com
for more information
or call 604-331-4471

What people say about Shane Gibson and his programs:

"I have outperformed all the other advisors hired in the last six months. This program was one of the best investments in myself I have ever made and I recommend it to anyone in sales who is serious about performing at a high level." *Antony McAleer, Financial Security Advisor, Freedom 55 Financial*

"...Your work with us has improved morale, contributed to a "sales focused" work environment, allowed most of our people to increase their personal compensation, and given our company a much healthier bottom line. Thank You." *Wayne LeGear, Vice-President – Auto Insurance – HUB International Insurance Services*

"I've been with the business school now for almost three years, and have seen quite a few presenters to the MBA class on a wide array of topics. I'd rank Shane as one of the strongest I've seen. Shane's presentation was very well received, and I'm sure we will want to have him back to give 'presentation skills presentations' to future classes." *Sauder School of Business, UBC*

Notes: